BRAND REWIRED

BRAND REWIRED

Connecting Intellectual Property, Branding,
and Creativity Strategy

Anne H. Chasser
Jennifer C. Wolfe, Esq., APR

WILEY

John Wiley & Sons, Inc.

Published by John Wiley & Sons, Inc., Hoboken, New Jersey.
Published simultaneously in Canada.

Brand Rewired™ is a registered trademark of Jennifer Wolfe.

Designations used by companies to distinguish their products are often claimed
as trademarks. In all instances where John Wiley & Sons, Inc., is aware of a claim,
the product names appear in initial capital or all capital letters. Readers, however,
should contact the appropriate companies for more complete information regarding
trademarks and registration.

For general information on our other products and services or for technical support,
please contact our Customer Care Department within the United States at
(800) 762-2974, outside the United States at (317) 572-3993, or fax at (317) 572-4002.

Wiley also publishes its books in a variety of electronic formats. Some content that
appears in print may not be available in electronic books. For more information about
Wiley products, visit our web site at www.wiley.com.

Library of Congress Cataloging-in-Publication Data:

Chasser, Anne H.
  Brand rewired: connecting intellectual property, branding, and creativity strategy /
Anne H. Chasser, Jennifer C. Wolfe.
      p. cm.
  Includes bibliographical references and index.
  ISBN 978-0-470-57542-0 (cloth/website)
  1. Product management. 2. Branding (Marketing) 3. Intellectual
property. 4. Strategic planning. I. Wolfe, Jennifer C. II. Title.
  HF5415.15.C46 2010
  658.8'27—dc22
                                                        2010003828

Printed in the United States of America

10 9 8 7 6 5 4 3 2 1

We dedicate this book to Tom and Wolfie.
Thank you for your love, support, and friendship.

Contents

Preface

This book is written for marketing, branding, and innovation leaders interested in improving the long-term return on investment of their branding and innovation plans. Whether you work in a large corporation, an agency environment, or an emerging or entrepreneurial company, if you are looking for a new way to add value to your innovation or branding process, this is the book for you.

To provide background on how this came about, in the fall of 2008, we began sharing stories on the innovation trends we continued to see in the intellectual property, venture capital, and entrepreneurial community. We found the discussion related to innovation and collaboration was centered on technology, research, development, and the creation of patents. There was limited discussion on the development of brands, trademarks, and other intellectual assets in the scope of innovation and intellectual property strategy.

Further, despite the widespread adoption of open innovation and collaboration as a way of thinking in contemporary business, there was still resistance to working as an interdisciplinary team with a shared vision. We continued to see silos and fiefdoms dominating day-to-day business with many touting the importance of collaboration, but few incorporating it into everyday practice.

We were certain that some companies were thinking about these issues and incorporating intellectual property strategy into the branding and innovation process. It seemed obvious to us that brands were critical to the success of most products and services. And protecting the brand with the right intellectual property is the key to capitalizing on that success over a long time. Every aspect of the way the consumer sees, touches, feels, and hears about the product is what really matters, particularly if it can be protected and last forever. It's not that technology isn't important, but it is only one piece of the puzzle.

With a shared interest in the subject, we started a literature review. We quickly learned that the landscape is saturated with traditional marketing and branding processes with varying twists and metaphors. In fact, a quick Amazon search of the key word *branding* produced more than 50,000 results at the time. There is no shortage of books written by and for marketing and branding professionals. Likewise, there is a proliferation of intellectual property or intellectual asset management books typically written by lawyers for other lawyers. And, in the open innovation sector, there is also a plethora of literature; however, it often focused on the research, development, and technology silo rather than bridging the gap into branding.

Intrigued, we set out to conduct preliminary interviews with innovation leaders at some of the world's biggest brands. Our goal: to test our theory that forward-thinking companies are finding ways to intersect strategic thinking about intellectual property with branding and innovation. Further, that doing so will result in a greater return on investment.

And so, our thesis was formed: If companies design into the innovation and brand development process strategic thinking about intellectual property, there is a longer term return on investment.

In *Brand Rewired*, we focus on the world's leading brands, interviewing their business leaders, innovators, and intellectual property strategists to learn how they are innovating, setting strategy, and achieving their end game. We interview the economists and valuation experts who place an economic value on brands in licensing and mergers and acquisition activity. Their quotes can be found throughout this book. We then build upon those trends and add another way of thinking about the branding process—a Brand Rewired.

Definitions

In our writing process, there are a few terms we used that we thought may be worth defining at the outset.

Brand Rewired: Design intellectual property strategy into the innovation and creative brand process from the beginning through the use of collaborative, multidisciplinary teams.

Brand Maestro: An executive leader responsible for facilitating the execution of branding and innovation plans to maximize return on investment while building powerful intellectual asset portfolios for the company. The Brand Maestro will possess a working understanding and knowledge of finance, marketing, intellectual property, consumer insights, risk management, corporate culture management, and group communication.

This leader may already exist in many organizations, but needs empowerment from top leadership to cross over various departments in order to create a profound and long-lasting impact on the branding strategy of the company.

Innovation 3.0: Innovation expands beyond new technologies and open innovation in the Research and Development department into the creation of new product lines, new brands, and new market spaces through intellectual asset strategy. Innovation 3.0 creates value while invention creates things.

New Economy 2010: New Economy in the late 1990s to early 2000s was all about businesses obtaining large cash infusions to rapidly build a web site or technology to leverage an exploding new market space. In 2010, it means streamlined overhead, reduced costs, more use of outside experts and outside resources, open and collaborative innovation, and consumer-driven products and services.

Acknowledgments

This journey began with a casual conversation and it continues, thanks to support, encouragement, and help from so many of colleagues, friends, and family members.

It was amazing for us to experience the willingness of so many people to help us with this project.

Special thanks to Gordon Smith, who took a look at our concept and immediately sent it Susan McDermott at John Wiley, our publisher. Susan, along with her team of Judy Howarth, Adrianna Johnson, and Melissa Lopez, have been invaluable throughout the process and especially during the final months of production.

David Stimson, Jackie Leimer, Steve Weinberg, and Robin Rolfe encouraged us early in the process. As recognized visionaries in trademark law and branding, they immediately understood the gap we were trying to fill. Craig Vogel understands the power of collaboration and as a designer, professor, and innovator values power and importance of early IP protection.

Our thought-leaders and interviewees inspired us with their insights and their willingness to share best practices in open innovation, branding, marketing and collaborative IP strategy. Special thanks to: J. Scott Evans, Nils Montan, Sandy Harbrecht, Kyle McQuaid, Gordon Smith, Scott Phillips, Jackie Leimer, David Stimson, Jeff Weedman, Steve Goers, Heidi Emanuel, Ruby Zefo, Kathy Selker, Gregg Marrazzo, Bill Price, Gail Lione, A.B. Cruz, Bob Wehling, Inger Eckert, Joanne Bischman, Vince Volpi, Sean Sauber, Bill Theimann, Benton Sauer, and Jerome McDonnell. Thanks too to everyone who encouraged us but was unable to participate in our interviews.

Comments and suggestions of our early "friendly readers," kept us focused and on course. Thanks to Margarita Keeton, Jackie Leimer, David Moyer, David Stimson, Liz Kennedy, Lisa Antolino, Craig Vogel, Margaret Swallow, Carol Spils, Jillian and Paul Darwish,

Ryan McKillen, Chris Allen, Linda Dunseath, and Ann Welsh. Special thanks go to our friends and colleagues at the International Trademark Association, especially Alan Drewsen and Dolores Hanna.

The Wolfe Law Firm team was amazing and worked with us throughout the process—editing, assembling, reviewing, researching and cataloging. We thank Emily Hamilton, Laurie Kunkel, Steve Jaeger, Cindy Bolden, and Lindsey Jaeger. Student interns John Litscher and Gabriose Keeton contributed their researching skills to our project.

To colleagues and fellow innovators at the University of Cincinnati, it's a pleasure to be associated with such a dynamic forward thinking institution. Design students Mike Sanders and Brooke Brandewie helped with the naming of our book while Matt Choto refined our graphic concepts. Finally, we are forever grateful to our families and loved ones, Bob and Jack Wolfe, Judy and Ed Ball, Tom Mantei, Katie and Nick Coakley, Tim and Stephen Chasser who all encouraged and believed in us every inch of the way. We love you and thank you.

CHAPTER 1

The Billion-Dollar Question

*At the beginning of the decade, Procter & Gamble had 10 billion-
dollar brands in its portfolio, brands that generate more than
one billion dollars in sales each year. Today, they have 23 of these
billion-dollar brands.*

— P&G 2009 Annual Report

*Google was formed in 1995 as a start-up company by a group of
Stanford students. Less than 10 years later, its brand is reported
to be valued at $100 billion.*

— Millward Brown Annual Brand Report 2009

How do Procter & Gamble, Google, and others like them build a
billion-dollar brand? They design strong intellectual property strategy into their innovation and branding processes through the power
of collaboration and interdisciplinary teams. In this book, we chron-
icle our discussions with the innovation, branding, and intellectual
property leaders from top global brands to share their ideas and
best practices in the next generation of branding and innovation.
Whether a company is maintaining a brand that has endured for
more than 100 years, such as Tide, or creating a new brand that

will capture the attention of the world, such as Google, a rewired branding process can provide key competitive advantages.

We ask the question: "How does a company ensure that when it invests in developing new technology, products, and services, the brand it builds to sell that product will have long-term staying power and produce a greater return on investment?"

Based upon our research and discussions with brand leaders, the key to economic success in developing and maintaining brands is to design intellectual property strategy into the creative and innovation process. This must occur from the beginning through the use of collaborative, multidisciplinary teams to effectively rewire the branding process.

Whether you are a brand manager inside a large corporation, working in an agency, or an entrepreneur, you will find that important trends are increasing the need to think about intersecting intellectual property strategy with the creative process. Thinking about intellectual property at the outset of the creative process means that you will have something with longer and more sustainable value. Additionally, changing accounting and finance principles mean your brand may be revalued each year. The right strategy to protect your brand can increase its value. If your brands are diminishing in value, they may have a bigger impact on the company than ever before.

The goal for most innovation or brand campaigns is to increase:

- Margin
- Market share
- Revenue
- Market value

In *The Game Changer* (2008), A.G. Lafley, former CEO of Procter & Gamble, preached what marketers have long touted—that we must innovate and create for consumer needs and wants in order to achieve an increase in margin, market share, revenue, and market value. But in the changing demands of the current economic climate, that approach alone may not be enough. In the future, companies must add another layer of thinking to the creative process.

Long-lasting intellectual property must also be the result of creativity and innovation activities. This requires an interdisciplinary approach from the start with an understanding of what it takes to create powerful and economically valuable intellectual property.

If we approach the brand process in this way, we can get the job done faster, utilizing fewer resources, reducing costs, and increasing the likelihood of success. To do so, some assumptions that permeate most companies must be changed and new processes embraced.

For example, most people think of patents when they hear the term *intellectual property*, which taints their thinking about the need to intersect it with the creative process. But intellectual property, as it relates to branding, includes protecting all aspects of the campaign. Just a few of the components that can be protected as valuable intellectual assets of the company include the following:

- Product name
- Logo
- Slogan
- Design of the product
- Design of the packaging
- Distinctive colors of the product or packaging
- Copy in the ad
- Script of the commercial
- Look and feel of the retail location or point of sale
- Distinctive sounds and smells associated with the product/campaign
- Music that accompanies the ad campaign
- Content created on the web site
- Every aspect in a branding campaign, if it is considered as an intellectual asset at the time of creation

These elements are protected by:

- Trademarks/trade dress
- Trade secrets—know-how
- Copyright
- Design patents

Thinking about intellectual property in the middle of the creative process or at the end of the process is too late. Protecting every facet of the campaign strategically means it can last longer, have a greater impact, and produce a higher return on investment for the company. It becomes an intellectual asset of the company to be used as leverage in obtaining financing and an important part of the market value, which affects stock prices.

Brand Rewired offers a unique approach to an otherwise age-old topic for branding, innovation, and marketing professionals.

- A brand strategy intersecting with an equally powerful intellectual property strategy produces a greater economic return and more rewards for brand project leaders.
- The elements of a strong intellectual property branding portfolio often mirror a strong branding campaign from a sales and marketing perspective.
- Failing to consider these important strategies can not only reduce the effectiveness of the value of the brand, but potentially expose the company to lawsuits and increased costs.
- The internal black box–silo mentality culture of organizations can impede the development and capitalization of innovation, branding, and intellectual property and ignore key opportunities.
- A multidisciplinary Brand Rewired approach will reduce costs and increase return on investment.

Our research includes discussions with executives; innovation, marketing, and branding professionals; trademark lawyers; intellectual property strategists; and professional intellectual asset valuation experts from leading worldwide companies including Procter & Gamble, General Mills, Intel, Harley-Davidson, Kimberly-Clark, Kodak, Yahoo!, Kraft Foods, Scripps Networks Interactive, and branding and advertising companies including J Walter Thompson (JWT), LPK, Northlich, and Interbrand.

The Evolution of the Silo—Rewired

To understand current thinking on innovation and branding, we started with historical research on the innovation trends that have occurred in contemporary companies since the early 1900s to understand how and why we have arrived where we are in 2010.

A short caveat about the term *innovation*, which has largely been used to address the creation of new ideas, technologies, or products from a scientific perspective: In 2007, Wayne Johnson, the vice president of university relations worldwide for Hewlett-Packard Company, defined it to mean the partnering of two or more companies with the government and universities to share products and ideas to develop a new, innovative item. We use it in a broader sense: innovation can come from anywhere and can mean any new way of thinking about your business or brand. *We view this as Innovation 3.0.* Innovation 3.0 expands beyond new technologies and open innovation in the research and development department into the creation of new product lines, new brands, and new market spaces through intellectual asset strategy. Innovation 3.0 creates value while invention creates things.

We found that a silo approach to doing business dominated the management philosophy of the leading branding companies for most of the twentieth century.

Figure 1.1 shows the silo approach and outlines what traditionally occurred for many years. Executive leadership set a general strategy for the company. The research and development (R&D) department was charged with creating new products or ideas for improvement in processes. Across industry divisions, scientists, engineers, developers, chemists, or others with specialized knowledge would develop new variations of products or services, often independent of marketing, research, or consumer input. At Procter & Gamble, it might be a new way to make a better diaper or soap dispenser. At Kraft Foods, it might be a new variation on a product package design or a better process for making cheese. At Apple, it might be a new application or design for its iconic line of products. You get the idea. Each company has its own set of new ideas that R&D can develop.

In this silo approach, R&D had an incentive, financially and otherwise, to create new products and services via patents filed. In fact, many companies offered lavish awards ceremonies and perks for those from R&D who generated the most (quantity, not quality) patents in a year. For many in R&D departments, a point of pride was the number of patents on which they were named an inventor.

Patent lawyers, too, have had an incentive to produce a certain number of patents per year. In this silo approach, R&D would produce many inventions and apply for the patents globally before the product moved into the monetization phase, where it could be rolled out to its target consumer. Although forward-thinking companies have moved away from this linear and quantitative approach,

Executive Leadership

Sets business strategy for growth of company.

Decides when to move beyond R&D and into commercial deployment.

Determines cost-benefit and risk analysis for moving forward with campaign.

Research & Development

Develops new products and services.

Reports to Executive Leadership providing recommendations.

Patent Counsel

Provides opinion on patentability/freedom to practice—applies for patents.

Marketing

Brand/Ad Agency

Creates branding and marketing campaigns for commercial deployment based upon consumer research.

Reports to Executive Leadership providing recommendations.

Trademark/Advertising Counsel

Provides opinion on whether campaign will infringe on rights of others and availability of trademarks—applies for trademarks.

Figure 1.1 The Silo Approach

the pitfall becomes obvious when looking at the return on investment in today's climate. As the cost to maintain patents globally skyrockets, the need to monetize that investment sooner becomes even more important. Yet, if the invention itself becomes obsolete shortly into its life cycle, becomes a source of lawsuits, or has limited to no commercial use, the return on that investment is dramatically diminished. This silo approach no longer produces the same economic return.

In this silo approach, the project crossed over the divide from R&D to marketing. As the marketing and branding team became involved, they worked their magic in crafting a message and a campaign to sell the product to the targeted consumer. At the end of the chain, trademark lawyers would get involved to register and protect the name, run clearance searches, and review advertising copy to ensure the company's exposure to lawsuits was minimal. Historically, most of the creative heavy lifting had been done at that point, and the trademark and advertising lawyer had limited power to advise on the strength or power of the brand or campaign as intellectual property. Instead, the intellectual property lawyer was relegated to clearing the name, slogan, or ad as "available" and as not likely to pose any threat of a lawsuit from some other company.

In this linear fashion, all of the parties worked in silos, each offering their expertise at a specific time in the product's life cycle, rarely working together in a collaborative manner. Territories, fiefdoms, and power struggles emerged in contemporary American companies throughout most of the twentieth century.

The Fiefdom Syndrome

According to Robert J. Herbold (2004), fiefdoms can form in many ways and for many reasons. They have long been a problem in corporations where they easily form when people have enduring faith in the isolationism of defending turf, maintaining the status quo, and looking out for themselves (individual or department interests) versus moving the organization forward at a larger level. When fiefdoms form at a group level inside a company where a small group of people centralize resistance around common tasks, responsibilities, or objectives, the damage can be irreparable.

This process worked for most of the twentieth century. It was modified and changed according to the current thinking of the day. During those years when the linear silo approach thrived, the largest companies dominated with a monopoly on access to capital and economies of scale to afford the best people in the world. Without many challengers and a wide-open marketplace, business was simpler and the linear process worked, tapping into each group's strengths in turn.

In the 1980s, a flurry of merger and acquisition activity began to occur, resulting in companies buying each other to obtain brands and technologies in order to dominate the marketplace and form mini-monopolies in product categories. As cultures merged in the perfect storm of activity, the silos, fiefdoms, and linear approach to development was further reinforced within these mega-companies.

In the last 10 to 15 years, however, this silo approach has slowly evolved and changes have begun to emerge. As the world became flat, a phrase coined by Thomas Friedman in his book *The World Is Flat*, global competition increased, and the need for greater return on investment became more important than ever. When global markets can compete with dramatically reduced overhead and increased margins, the need for more focused development activities that actually produce results is paramount. U.S. companies quickly became aware that if they couldn't cut costs or increase market share, they wouldn't survive.

Consumers also became more powerful than ever during this time period. For decades, companies had dictated what would be developed and then created ad campaigns to convince consumers they needed it. In the age of Facebook, YouTube, blogs, Twitter, Yahoo!, and Google, consumers are in the driver's seat, picking and choosing what they want, when they want it, and abandoning those companies who fail to heed their demands.

Additionally, the technology age and the ability to tap into resources better, faster, and cheaper mean that smaller companies can compete with the big companies without the high barrier to entry that created the monopolies of the first half of the twentieth century. Thus, the emergence of venture capital firms in the 1990s, pumping money into entrepreneurial companies with the latest and greatest ideas, meant these small giants could suddenly challenge Goliath in a battle of the marketplace. Goliath has since realized,

1900–1980
American corporations dominate the global marketplace in an old school research and development linear model with limited competition and the economies of scale to hire the best people, believing deeply in the philosophy "if it's not invented here, it's not a good idea."

1980s
A flurry of merger and acquisition activity results in mini-monopolies within product categories. As cultures merged in the perfect storm of activity, silos and fiefdoms emerged to protect turf and reinforced a linear approach to innovation and development, regardless of how costly it might be to the company.

1990s
The world becomes flat with the onset of the Internet and the ability to collaborate with anyone anywhere in the world. Coupled with changing worldwide economic conditions, American companies no longer dominate to the global marketplace and begin to face competition from companies that can do the same thing but with less overhead and higher margins.

1990s
With the access to resources afforded by technology, entrepreneurial companies can compete with the corporate giants in the marketplace of ideas. Venture capital companies form to pump capital into these start-ups. The sleeping giants awaken and realize they, too, must tap into ideas from the outside to survive.

2000s
Consumers take charge, no longer at the mercy of an ad campaign to convince them they need something. With the proliferation of consumer-generated media and in-demand services, companies now must heed the call of their customers. Yahoo!, Google, YouTube, Facebook, Twitter, and blogs emerge giving consumers all the power. Companies realize they must listen to their customers or they won't have any.

2008
The world financial markets melt down resulting in bailouts from the U.S. government of the largest financial institutions in the world. Access to capital becomes limited and constrained with no signs of improvement in the foreseeable future. To access the limited available capital in an ever increasing global competitive landscape, companies must ensure they maintain strong balance sheets and predictable cash flow. No longer can companies afford a linear old school research and development process, but must innovate and connect to their customers in a more meaningful way that results in economic value.

in the development of open innovation, that it, too, needs entrepreneurial ideas to survive.

Most recently, the economic meltdown of the financial markets in 2008 meant that access to capital would become more and more constrained.

In what began as a revolution in response to the world becoming flat, the need for intellectual property strategy has become of paramount importance. Companies have recognized that a more fluid and interdisciplinary approach that is laser-focused on consumer needs is required to achieve better results.

Modern companies no longer have the luxury of indulging unfocused development that recognizes quantity over quality and sunk costs that cannot produce the required return on investment. They must implement better tools in order to survive the coming trends in the financial and consumer markets.

As the information age evolved from Web 1.0 to the social and collaborative Web 2.0, leading companies began to form interdisciplinary teams. These teams work in a collaborative manner to develop new products and services centered on consumers and their wants and needs in order to dominate the marketplace.

The term *innovation* began, in many instances, to replace *research and development,* and the need and desire to innovate with external resources became accepted, leading to the term coined by Henry Chesbrough, *open innovation.* Now, many companies employ chief innovation officers or VPs of open innovation. These innovation leaders have many functions to ensure their company sets strategies and practices in place to tap into the global marketplace of ideas, shares knowledge, and improves its competitive edge. In fact, in 2003, Aranoff and FitzPatrick noted that companies have set a policy to abandon the "not invented here" syndrome (NIH). NIH was founded on the theory that if we didn't think of it, it's not a good idea. Instead, most companies now understand that good ideas can come from anywhere, and that it's what you do with those good ideas that really matters. And so we arrive in the New Economy. Companies must do more with less and produce even greater return on investment faster to compete and survive.

With a brief understanding of how we got to where we are, it's time to look forward. What new approach or way of thinking can add an additional layer of value to a company?

Figure 1.2 illustrates the Brand Rewired approach. Innovation, branding, consumer insights, intellectual property, and execution are all part of a fluid process designed to achieve one common goal: the desired return on investment. This requires constant multidisciplinary planning, communication, execution, and follow-up with an emphasis on the creation of powerful intellectual property in tandem

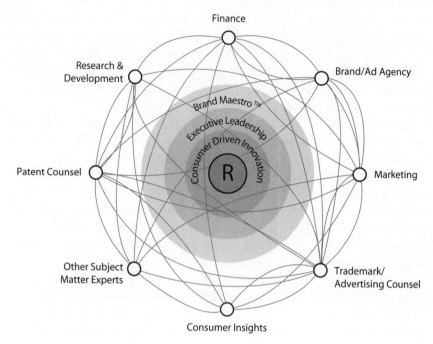

Finance

Research & Development

Brand/Ad Agency

Brand Maestro ™
Executive Leadership
Consumer Driven Innovation

Patent Counsel

R

Marketing

Other Subject Matter Experts

Trademark/ Advertising Counsel

Consumer Insights

Figure 1.2   Brand Rewired

with a powerful brand. The requirements for achieving powerful intellectual property and a powerful brand are, typically, the same.

At the center of this process is consumer-driven innovation. Innovating based upon consumers' needs, desires, and wants must be at the cornerstone of your innovation and branding, whatever your industry and whoever your consumer. *Even if the consumers do not yet know they need your product or service or that they will connect forever with your brand, you must understand the consumer fully in order to succeed.* Consumers may not have known that they needed a computer at home, but Macintosh helped them understand that they did in the 1980s, creating a whole new market for the computer industry. Apple sought its consumer base by understanding what its consumers do at home and creating a product to fit those needs.

As new ideas and innovation form at the consumer level, executive leadership sets a strategy for the company and creates the cultural tone that is essential for a Brand Rewired approach to be successful. To ensure success, we advocate that a leader emerge in contemporary companies, a Brand Maestro. A Brand Maestro is skilled at facilitation and group communication in leading multi-disciplinary teams, but also knowledgeable in multiple disciplines—intellectual asset strategy, consumer insights, innovation, branding, communication, intellectual property, and strategic planning, with a focus on building a powerful brand and intellectual property portfolio for the company.

The Brand Maestro's role is to flawlessly execute a brand and intellectual property strategy that delivers the expected return on investment through a multidisciplinary team.

The Brand Maestro ensures that the end game or goal is always at the forefront, the consumer is always at the center, and that all of the subject matter experts—branding, sales, market research, consumer insights, patent lawyers, trademark lawyers—are contributing in a collaborative manner at the right time to have the greatest impact with the lowest amount of costs.

The Brand Maestro, through a Brand Rewired approach, intersects each of these experts at the right moment throughout the process to deliver better results. The Brand Maestro likely already exists in most companies in some form or another. We crystallize the process and the role that is needed to maximize return on investment in a Brand Rewired approach.

At the end of our studies and research, we found that unquestionably, designing intellectual property strategy into the innovation and branding process would lead to a higher return on investment. Equally important, the key to accomplishing that goal is to utilize interdisciplinary teams. The tools needed to do so include the following steps:

- Leadership of the company sets a vision and creates a culture that fosters and embraces multidisciplinary teams.
- A process is put in place to emphasize strong intellectual asset strategy and management in tandem with the creative and innovation process through the use of multidisciplinary teams.
- Common goals, collaboration, and teamwork are rewarded through financial and nonfinancial recognition.

What's Ahead?

In this introductory chapter, we have illustrated the changing trends in innovation, development, and branding from a linear, silo approach to a collaborative model with an emphasis on intellectual property. Our story will continue by understanding what is of paramount importance to every company undertaking any innovation, development, or branding—how does that activity result in economic value?

From there, we look to understand what happens in the creative process and how to simultaneously create more powerful and robust intellectual assets that achieve the end game.

We then evaluate key trends that are driving business decisions and are highlighted in popular and contemporary business literature.

Armed with an understanding of what's occurring in the marketplace and driving decision making, we tap into a case study to examine what happens in the silo approach. Utilizing their story, we analyze what can go wrong in today's marketplace when the silo approach prevails.

We then turn the case study around, taking the same journey but with a Brand Rewired, collaborative approach emphasizing intellectual property strategy, analyzing what can go right, how to overcome the challenges that are inevitable, and demonstrating the power of collaboration driven by clear strategy.

We recap what is needed in a Brand Maestro and how to create an intellectual property, branding, and innovation strategy that is linked directly to achieving the end game—economic rewards.

Finally, we close with a brief history of the companies we researched and the leaders we interviewed with an emphasis on how these companies are tackling the challenge of working in multidisciplinary teams.

> Business—more than any other occupation—is a continual dealing with the future; it is a continual calculation, an instinctive exercise in foresight.
>
> HENRY LUCE

Chapter Highlights

- The key to economic success in developing and maintaining brands is to design intellectual property strategy into the creative and innovation process from the beginning through the use of collaborative, multidisciplinary teams—to effectively rewire the branding process.

Most innovation or brand campaigns are valued based upon increased margin, increased market share, increased revenue, increased market value, or some combination of the above. Every aspect of a campaign can be protected: name, logo, slogan, product design, package design, distinctive color schemes, music for the ad campaign, copy for the ad campaign, script for commercials, content on web sites, look and feel of a retail location or point of purchase. Every aspect of a branding campaign can be protected and can endure if it is considered when it is created. This gives it a higher return on investment. Leadership must set a vision and create a culture that fosters and embraces multidisciplinary teams. A process must be put in place to facilitate multidisciplinary teams. Common goals, collaboration, and teamwork are rewarded through financial and nonfinancial recognition.

- For many years, the largest companies in the world were able to dominate the marketplace by their size, capital power, and ability to leverage and tap into resources, easily boxing out competitive threats. This facilitated and supported a linear way of developing new ideas, technologies, and brands. This way of thinking dominated management and leadership styles of leading companies from the industrial revolution through most of the twentieth century, creating very linear processes with silos and fiefdoms controlling.

  With the flurry of mergers and the acquisition activity of the 1980s, corporate cultures were merged, further reinforcing the silo phenomenon in what were now mega-companies.

- The technology age arrived in the last part of the twentieth century with an increasing acceleration of change in the business landscape, forcing company leadership to face new challenges and competitive threats unlike those at any time in its history, increasing costs to do business and diminishing margins.

  As global marketplaces, once relatively untapped, became competitive threats, the previously dominant companies now faced competitors that could do the same thing but with significantly less overhead and much higher margins.

- At the same time, technology leveled the playing field by creating access to resources that didn't exist in previous years, and entrepreneurial companies, often armed with venture capital backing, could now compete head to head with the largest companies in the world, putting an increasing demand on the need for fresh, new ideas.

    Consumers also became more powerful than ever before. For decades, companies dictated what would be developed and then created ad campaigns to convince consumers they needed it. Now, consumers are in the driver's seat, picking and choosing what they want, when they want it, and abandoning those companies who fail to heed their demands.

- The largest companies in the world recognized in the 1990s that they could no longer function in silos and develop ideas in a linear fashion and began to evolve into a more collaborative model with consumer needs at the center, driving the process.

- Then as the economic meltdown occurred in 2008, companies recognized that access to capital would be constrained, transparency of executive activity would be demanded, and the need to maximize return on investment on a longer term basis would become paramount to survival.

- With these many factors putting significant pressure on contemporary companies, the need to innovate, develop, and brand in a smarter way has been causing the old silo approach to management to evolve into a new, collaborative model—a Brand Rewired.

2

Value Is in the Eye of the Beholder

To understand more about the latest trends in innovation, branding, intellectual property strategy, and creativity, and how they intersect in leading global companies, we decided it might be a good idea to start with the end game. After all of the hard work, what is the value proposition? *What creates a better return on investment for the company?*

The answer was ultimately very simple: Build something that can continue to produce revenue for a long time. The details behind it are a bit more complex.

There are several important trends driving the need for anyone involved in branding to better understand how intellectual assets are valued. With an increasing percentage of a company's market value based upon its brand, strategic thinking about how the brand becomes valuable intellectual property owned by the company and valued in the marketplace must be introduced into the conversation.

> Think of your brand as a "bank account," something that you build up over time by making deposits. It grows and compounds through increased interest, investment, and attention. During lean periods, you may need to make withdrawals and rely on the strength of your brand. If you keep making withdrawals and never add to it, however, then you may find the brand is not as strong as it once was.
>
> DAVID STIMSON,
> Chief Trademark Counsel, Kodak, and
> Former President, International Trademark Association

Driving Trends in Intellectual Asset Valuation—Why It Matters to You

We had the opportunity to speak with Gordon Smith and Scott Phillips, widely recognized as leading global intellectual asset valuation experts, and Jeff Weedman, vice president of global business development of Procter & Gamble, widely recognized as a thought leader in innovation. Smith is the one of the most published authors on intellectual property valuation; lectures globally to prestigious trade organizations, including the World Intellectual Property Organization; and is currently consulting and teaching extensively in growing markets such as Singapore, India, and China. Phillips leads Charles River Associates' trademark practice; has lectured and written extensively on the topic of valuation of brands, tax matters, and transitional activities; and was named by *Intellectual Asset Management* magazine as one of the "IAM 250—The World's Leading IP Strategists." Weedman is highly sought after as a thought leader in open innovation. In his leadership role at P&G, he launched an entrepreneurial licensing department charged with the commercialization of P&G's treasure trove of patents, trademarks, and know-how. Now transformed into a robust global business development organization, the group has a broad mission to create value through intellectual property management, including enabling Connect + Develop^SM—P&G's open innovation strategy that looks to access external technologies, "cooked products," capabilities, and business propositions. In our in-depth conversations, Smith, Phillips, and Weedman indicate there are several trends driving the importance of intellectual asset value to global companies: (1) emerging countries in branding as a rising competitive threat, (2) the power of the balance sheet, and (3) stronger intellectual assets making better brands and better products at a lower cost.

Emerging Countries in Branding as a Rising Competitive Threat

First, the companies in emerging countries of the world, such as the BRIC countries (Brazil, Russia, India, and China) are no longer satisfied to be contract manufacturers and low-cost offshore solutions to Western companies looking to reduce overhead. They aspire to join the world leaders in the creation of technology and in building brands around their innovative ideas. Smith, who consults in countries such as Singapore and in Southeast Asia, advises: "You must have a brand. If you don't build a brand, you don't have anything that is sustainable. Technology is good and important, but it will be obsolete relatively quickly. A brand, however, can last forever and serve as an umbrella under which new products and services can be introduced."

As emerging companies set their sights on being world leaders not only in manufacturing for other brands, but in creating and building their own global brands, they are focused on one fundamental characteristic of great brands: how they are valued. *And one of the key characteristics that give a brand more value is its strength as intellectual property.*

When emerging companies hire experts like Smith and Phillips to train, advise, and counsel on what makes a valuable brand, their answer is simple. Every intellectual asset, whether a patent, trade secret, trademark, brand, design, or other technology, is valued in a structurally similar process:

- How much income is it generating?
- What is the pattern of income production?
- How long can that continue?
- What is the risk it won't materialize as predicted due to obsolescence, dilution, or market changes?

A valuable brand is protected by intellectual property in order to last a long time and produce a lot of income with low risk of dilution and quality recognition associated with the brand. Our experts advise companies that they must build a brand around their technology so that as the technology changes, the brand continues to build in value. They do not discount the importance of technology, but advise that because most technology is outdated, if not obsolete, often before a patent can even issue, companies must compete in the battle of the brands.

The established branding companies must be prepared for continued and new competitive threats and be mindful of what counsel is being provided to those competitive threats. If these emerging companies are branding with the end game of better valuation in mind and stronger intellectual property to protect those brands, then savvy established brands will also build brands with stronger intellectual property value.

The Balance Sheet as Borrowing Power

The second trend driving an interest in brand value is a shift in accounting principles both in the United States and globally, related to the treatment of intellectual assets. The trend is simple:

- Most companies derive borrowing power from the strength of the balance sheet.
- Each year, acquired intellectual assets (i.e., brands, patents, trademarks, trade secrets, copyrights) must be valued. If the value has decreased, then the value on the balance sheet is decreased, thereby reducing borrowing power and market valuation.
- In this economic climate with limited capital available, businesses cannot afford to lose value or borrowing power.
- Unlike any time ever before, what the branding team does to increase or decrease brand value has a direct impact on the company's financial standing.

Why is this trend occurring? Our experts explain that in the 1980s, after a surge of merger and acquisition activity, the generally accepted accounting principles (also known as GAAP) were modified such that U.S. corporations that buy other corporations, including their brands, must state the fair value of any intangible assets on their balance sheet at the time of acquisition and annually thereafter. In June 2001, the Financial Accounting Standards Board (FASB), another governing body providing standards for financial reporting, also issued accounting standards, which require the purchase price allocation following an acquisition to define fair value as it relates to intellectual assets.

Historically, companies were required to amortize intellectual assets annually on their balance sheets. Most often, brand values were lumped together with "goodwill" that was to be amortized over their useful lives, but that period could not exceed 40 years. Keep in mind that the balance sheet is one of the tools used by lenders to determine the borrowing power of a company.

Today, acquired brands must be identified and valued, but they can be assigned an "indefinite life," and that characteristic exempts these assets from amortization and the steady decrease in balance sheet value under the previous accounting rules.

However, the recent shift in policy brings with it the requirement that each year a company must value its acquired intellectual assets and report their current fair market value. If the brand or intellectual asset has lost value, the value is reduced by that amount, negatively affecting the company's balance sheet.

This is referred to by the experts as "impairment." This means that in an era of reduced availability of capital, depreciating assets on your balance sheet will diminish your company's ability to borrow money and obtain necessary capital. It also reduces market valuation and thereby stock prices in the ups and downs of day-to-day Wall Street analysis.

Most market and brand managers recognize that the market value of the company rests in large part on the value of the brand as stated by these valuation experts. But, with a deeper understanding of how these professional valuators will value your brand's performance, you can improve your performance. Adding a layer of strategic thinking about intellectual property to the brand creation process will produce a higher long-term return on investment in the work that branding professionals provide.

According to a *BusinessWeek* report (July 23, 2009), 59 percent of top executives said the brand represents more than 40 percent of a company's market capitalization. Other sources suggest this number may be even larger. According to the BP Council (2009), the World Intellectual Property Organization (WIPO) reports that 80 percent of corporate value today is represented by intangible assets.

Stronger Intellectual Assets Make for Better Brands and Better Products

The result of considering intellectual property strategy at the outset of the innovation and branding process is simply a better way of doing things. By understanding the intellectual asset's value or pitfalls, as it may be, a company leader can make better, more strategic decisions that cost the company less money (i.e., a higher return on investment), which will ultimately result in a higher valuation.

All too often, exorbitant amounts of money can be spent on researching, developing, creating, and testing a product, a brand, or a campaign only to find out that it either can't be used or isn't of significantly greater value that what is already out there. Worse, it may result in a lawsuit from either the government or another large global company. These are all intellectual property issues. The result is a lot of money being spent without the ability to recapture it over a long enough period of time.

By considering intellectual property at the beginning of the creative process, costs can be reduced and the return on investment increased. It's really that simple. How many times have millions been spent on a campaign, only to find out the product isn't really that distinctive or different from what else is out there or can't be protected globally so it is easily replicated without recourse? Or it violates FTC guidelines or another's rights and results in a lawsuit? Factoring in the intellectual asset value and intellectual property issues earlier in the process will not only eliminate those costs, but will also ensure that the result is longer and more easily protectable value and power in a global marketplace.

> Using internal resources alone limits capabilities and opportunities. If we can collaborate and partner with others and also leverage external intellectual property, we have more knowledge to make better decisions.
>
> Leveraging external experts can often provide broader perspective and an outside view less encumbered in the status quo. Ask them to tear apart your product or campaign as if they were a competitor or to show you where there are weaknesses in what you have created. I would rather know up front where there are problems in the claims in our ad campaign, where our brand could be more powerful, how it could be copied or diluted, or how our newest product feature patents can be circumvented. If I ask the right questions of the right people upfront, I find the weaknesses and make our products or advertising stronger or be better prepared for competitors before we go to market— that can make a big difference.
>
> JEFF WEEDMAN,
> Vice President, Global Business
> Development, Procter & Gamble

The Driving Trends behind the Increasing Value of Intellectual Assets

- Emerging companies and competitive threats with more powerful intellectual property.

- The balance sheet as borrowing power.
- Stronger intellectual assets make for better brands and better products.

If you want to be another Donald Trump, you need to learn how to appraise real estate, because you need to know what drives value. If you want to be a leader in any global industry, you need to understand how intellectual assets are valued. Ninety percent of the value of many companies is driven by intellectual assets.

GORDON SMITH,
Professor, Franklin Pierce Law Center, and Chair, AUS, Inc.

When and How Intellectual Assets Are Valued

With an understanding of trends driving the need for regular valuation of intellectual assets, it is important to understand what typically would drive the need for a valuation, as well as standard methods for valuing intellectual assets. Generally, companies will value their brands for a few key reasons.

Financial Reporting Requirements. Annual valuations are required to adjust the value of acquired intangibles on the balance sheet.

Tax Savings. Many companies will utilize a subsidiary IP holding company in order to derive specific tax savings.

Royalty Income. As many companies expand globally, they often seek to license their brands to third parties to expand rapidly through existing distribution channels. This requires a valuation in order to calculate the appropriate royalty.

Joint Ventures. As companies evaluate contributing a brand to a joint venture, a value must be placed on the brand in order to negotiate the best possible deal.

Mergers and Acquisitions. As companies position for a sale or merger with another company, the value of the brand must be determined. For entrepreneurs, the all-important exit event is an important reason to pay attention to the value proposition.

Companies want to have their brands valued for differing reasons: financial reporting requirements, to take advantage of certain tax savings through an IP holding company, to calculate a royalty rate, to place a value on something being contributed to joint ventures, or to prepare for merger and acquisition activity. Sometimes, it is simply that a marketing department wants to quantify the value of a brand that has been created. While the reason for the valuation may slightly change our approach, the bottom line is always the same: What cash flow does the brand generate, and how long is that sustainable? When we approach a valuation, we consider all aspects, the marketing, the brand awareness, the legal strength, and most importantly, the positive net cash flow it creates.

SCOTT PHILLIPS,
Vice President and Trademark
Practice Leader, Charles River Associates

As the valuation expert moves into the process, he or she carefully evaluates a number of factors in order to arrive at those that translate to economic value. There are several approaches to valuing intellectual assets. Historically, assets, particularly intangible assets, might be valued based upon their cost to acquire or create rather than their economic value to the company. This breaks down into a simple definition:

Value = price agreed between a willing buyer and seller

or

Value = present value of a future economic benefit

Cost = specific price paid for goods or services at a particular point in time

While we all can understand cost, value is something that is constantly changing. There are several methods of valuing assets generally, and more specifically intellectual assets. It is important to understand that valuation professionals will look at each method and often blend these various results into a conclusion providing the present-day value for the asset.

To start, however, it may be helpful to define in more detail what comprises an intellectual or intangible asset.

- *Patents* include all issued and pending patents for technologies, inventions, processes, and methods eligible for patent protection. Patents may also include certain design patents on unique packaging designs.
- *Trademarks and Trade Dress* include names of products, slogans, taglines, product designs, logos, colors, smells, sounds, package designs—for example, the look and feel of a restaurant or retail location.
- *Trade Secrets* include all technologies not protected by patents, know-how, processes, training procedures, and other tools, techniques, and secrets used by a business that it maintains as confidential. The term *knowledge management* refers to managing the vast amount of company knowledge that has been compiled over its history, most of which can be protected.
- *Copyrights* include advertising campaigns, stories, web site copy, artistic renderings, characters, music, user-generated content, web content and submissions, and other ideas reduced to tangible written form.
- *Domain Names* include the exclusive right to use the domain name, including second-level domain names.
- *Goodwill* encompasses all of the other components of a brand—consumers' emotional connection to the brand, their loyalty, their experience, their history with the product—all of the reasons why consumers will buy a specific brand are housed in the intangible asset of goodwill, commonly known as the power of the brand.

Although many of you may be familiar with the basic valuation principles, it is helpful to review these methods of valuing intellectual assets used by professional valuators in contrast to the formula often used in the annual "Most Powerful Brand" lists or a marketing approach to brand value.

Market Approach

In real estate, stocks, bonds, or commodities, there are active markets that can easily provide comparable fair market value for a property of similar characteristics. For intangible assets, however, there is a limited base of comparable intangible assets from which to run a comparison. Evaluating the acquisition price or licensing royalty rates, to the extent known, of other similar brands can prove helpful for the valuation professional, but is not definitive. Prudent valuation professionals will conduct diligent searches of known databases for research about similar licensing or transactions involving similar intellectual assets to understand the market rate for such assets. They will seek to reconcile any differences or variables to arrive at a conclusive fair market comparable value to other known transactions in the marketplace. This is one method of valuation. It is typically not used as the sole indicator of value, but rather used to complement the income method and provide additional support or discretion in the valuation process.

Cost-Based Approach

A cost-based approach will define the value based upon the total historic costs for development or for replacement of the asset (either to purchase or reconstruct). This approach rarely is effective, because there is no direct correlation between the investment made and the anticipated return. Some brands may cost more than they can derive in value. Others may cost significantly less than they can derive in value. A cost-based approach is not effective in determining value. When conducting the cost-based approach, however, the professional will evaluate the various costs incurred in innovation, research, development, marketing, design, legal, and all operational costs associated with creating the intellectual asset. Some professionals will also factor in opportunity costs suffered to develop intellectual assets in this process (i.e., it may take years to build the intellectual value and in that time other opportunities were lost, resulting in a direct cost). Similarly, the professional may look at replacement costs to acquire a similar intangible asset, much like in the comparable approach.

Finally, the cost or replacement method will be offset due to any functional, technological, or market obsolescence. In other words, if the intellectual asset no longer can produce revenue at the anticipated levels, then it has become obsolete or suffered some level of obsolescence. Technological obsolescence may arise by other technologies surpassing it in the marketplace. Market obsolescence may result from changes in market conditions such that the product, service, or brand is no longer desired in the marketplace or that it has been diluted or diminished in the marketplace. Obviously, the more staying power the brand has, the less likely it is to be affected by an obsolescence adjustment in the valuation process.

Income Approach

The income approach is the most widely used as it values the present value of future income or the expectation value of the intellectual asset. This requires the professional to estimate the expected rate of return offset by the risk of uncertainty. Most frequently, this approach evaluates the gross revenue or cash flow generated by the revenue-generating activity of the intellectual asset. Keep in mind that most intellectual assets generate revenue in one of the following ways:

- Direct sales of the products to consumers
- Exclusive distribution agreements with third-party resellers providing margin on the sale of the products
- License agreements with third-party resellers producing royalties on the use of the assets

In the income approach, professionals will evaluate the estimated normalized measure of economic income for one period (perhaps one year or five years or more) and then divide that by an appropriate investment rate of return. This is referred to as a direct capitalization rate. Alternatively, the professional may project a measure of economic income for several specific time periods into the future and then convert it into a present value by the use of a present value discount rate. The present value discount rate is recognized as a yield capitalization rate over the expected term of economic income.

An important point to note is that one of the key factors used in the income approach is the determination of any risk factors that might disrupt or diminish the expected future revenue-generating activity.

The two key questions then become:

1. What is the probability of the favorable economic event occurring?
2. What is the payoff if the event occurs?

There are many factors that can diminish the value of intellectual assets, including the following:

Risk Factors for Future Value of Intellectual Assets

- Can the product become obsolete due to new technologies?
- How long will the exclusivity of the asset last? Patents will last 20 years, if not obsolete, yet trademarks can endure forever.
- Can the trademark be protected globally? How strong is the trademark? Unique, fanciful, nondescriptive marks are stronger.
- Is the trademark at risk of dilution (i.e., a weakening connection between the product and the company)?
- Is there more than one form of intellectual property protecting the brand or the asset such that if one is diminished another may take its place (i.e., a design patent plus trademark protection for a unique package design)?
- Will counterfeiting hurt sales activities or diminish the power of the brand?
- Is there potential for costly lawsuits based upon perceived infringement that will disrupt anticipated margins?
- Versatility of the brand can be very important. If it is tied closely to a narrowly defined product or service, then its life equals the product/service's life. If it is versatile, it can survive the demise of the original use.

While we will provide more details on the components of intellectual property that can be protected in Chapter 3, it is important to understand that failing to consider dilution and risk factors in the value of these components can hurt the ultimate valuation.

Economic Use/Brand Equity Approach

The brand equity approach adds another layer of thinking to the income approach and is not widely used as a sole source of value prediction, but it is an important method worth consideration. This approach is driven by brand equity measures combined with financial measures. It is more of a marketing function than an economic one. The marketing component values the consumer demand that translates into revenue through purchase volume, price, and frequency, as well as long-term consumer demand. The financial component then evaluates the expected future earnings discounted using a discount rate, as in the income approach. This method combines the two into one value prediction.

This approach factors in predicting the effect of marketing and investment strategies, determining and assessing communication budgets, calculating the return on brand investment, assessing new opportunities in brand investment, and tracking brand value management. A series of steps are taken to understand market segmentation, financial forecasts, demand predictions, competitive benchmarking, and predictions to arrive at a brand value calculation. This area of valuation is expanding in interest as marketing professionals seek to understand other means of valuing their assets. Regardless of the tools and techniques in place, the income approach will always be a balancing factor in understanding brand equity and the marketing value placed on consumer demand in the marketplace.

Research-Based Approach

A final approach is noneconomic in nature and is used in marketing rather than finance. Although it is not likely to be reflected on the company balance sheet, it is worth noting. A research-based method will measure consumer behavior and attitudes that impact the economic performance of a brand. These will seek to explain, interpret, and measure consumer perception and purchasing behavior related to consumer knowledge and beliefs about the brand. A brand can perform strongly in the indicators related to consumer behavior, but due to other issues, not perform strongly in delivering financial value and shareholder value. Brand equity, under this approach, is measured on five dimensions: familiarity, uniqueness, relevance, popularity, and quality. The five dimensions determine the significance of the brand and then cross analyze it with the relevance of the brand category to the consumer and price as a perceived value. The brand health is then an understanding of brand equity benchmarked against category involvement and value assessment.

A final key point in understanding the value of the brand to the company is to recognize that increasingly these intangible assets of the company are being utilized as collateral to obtain important capital fueling the growth of the company. Experts from the World Intellectual Property Organization have estimated that global commerce in the emerging IP asset class is worth an estimated

$300 billion worldwide. While many details surround the security interests related to pledging intellectual assets, the trend of tapping into these valuable resources will continue.

Increasing the Return on Investment of Your Next Project

Branding professionals who want to set themselves apart will understand what creates value in one of the most powerful intellectual assets of their company—the brand. Brand equity, as Smith and Phillips state, has no meaning when it comes to valuing the asset. It is a "touchy-feely" marketing term used to equate to something intangible. Market value, however, is another thing. "I can quantify the market value associated with a brand," says Smith.

When we asked our experts what advice they would give to a brand manager looking to bolster the market value of a brand, they replied:

- Reduce risk associated with the brand; ensure the quality remains consistent and the goodwill from consumers remains consistent. Don't let anything bad happen to that goodwill.
- Ensure as long a life as possible. Prevent and stop infringers, prevent counterfeiting, avoid becoming generic in the marketplace, pay attention to competitors. There is a belief that a trademark or trade secret will last forever, but only if appropriate measures are taken.
- Ensure that the brand remains worthwhile for the consumers—do whatever is needed to ensure that they continue to want to pay a slightly higher margin for your brand over someone else's.

> I often hear people talk about protection. Protection is a by-product of building a valuable brand, not the strategy. What I want to hear is more about how to exploit the brand with protection being a mere component of that plan.
>
> GORDON SMITH,
> Professor, Franklin Pierce Law Center, and Chair, AUS, Inc.

Exploitation of the brand requires some brand integrity. How do you ensure that the quality of the goodwill associated with the brand is maintained?

If you dissect what a brand really is and what it means, it is a belief by consumers that they will receive a certain benefit from the product—whether it is the status of the label, the feel of the fine quality, or the service when they arrive. This is all part of the brand. And each component can be protected by intellectual property to ensure longer term economic value. This protection and ability to exploit at the lowest possible cost provides the return on investment.

To create economic value, these factors must be maintained. They can be maintained with a strong intellectual property strategy tied to a strong brand strategy. Equally important, they build the framework for a return on investment.

The increasing recognition of the value of intangibles came with continuous increases in the gap between companies' book values and their stock market valuations, as well as sharp increases in premiums above the stock market value that were paid in mergers and acquisitions in the late 1980s. Some brands have also demonstrated astonishing durability. Jan Lindemann (2009) noted that the world's most valuable brand, Coca-Cola, is more than 118 years old, and the majority of the world's most valuable brands have been around for more than 60 years. This compares with an estimated average life span for a corporation of 25 years or so. Many brands have survived a string of different corporate owners. It has been shown that a portfolio weighted by the brand values of the Best Global Brands performs significantly better than Morgan Stanley's global MSCI index and the American-based S&P 500 index.

This is an important point. Real strategy in developing the brand as a powerful asset is about more than just asking the lawyer how to protect it. It is about a comprehensive plan that mandates multidisciplinary thinking to achieve the factors defined here in how to value a brand economically. There is no way only a branding or creative person, only a lawyer, or only an innovation expert can know all of these things at the level needed. As emerging companies start to play in the space and are building their teams with best practices, contemporary leading companies must be prepared to rethink the way they do things if they want to succeed.

You may notice that much of this discussion has been focused on brands and the components of brands, whereas a large part of a company's intellectual assets are rooted in its technology and patent portfolio.

While we in no way mean to diminish the value of a strong patent portfolio, many companies have begun to recognize that:

- Only a small percentage of all issued patents are actually in use in the marketplace.
- The cost to maintain these patents globally is growing exponentially.
- Many companies now evaluate whether to continue to maintain patents and seek to understand where the greater value proposition and return on investment exists.

Further, while certain technologies or patents can box out competitors exclusively for the 20-year period of time, creating a virtual monopoly, in most technology categories, the patents behind the technology are obsolete and improved upon before the patents even issue globally. This results in a large black hole of legal expenses to protect and maintain patents globally for a limited return on investment.

Don't get us wrong—innovation of technology is critical, as are the right patents. It just needs another layer of intellectual property to get the most bang for the buck—it needs a brand and a powerful one at that. The experts weighed in on this issue.

> Brands are generally more valuable than specific technologies, because while much technology is out of date in a short period of time, most brands have long future lives.
>
> SCOTT PHILLIPS,
> Vice President and Trademark
> Practice Leader, Charles River Associates

> The success of new product innovation at our company is evaluated in three ways:
>
> 1. Incremental Revenue—meaning it is new revenue, not replacement of existing volume
> 2. Profitable
> 3. Sustainable in the marketplace
>
> HEIDI EMANUEL,
> Senior Innovation Officer, General Mills

The single most important outcome of all innovation activity is demonstrating value.

STEVE GOERS,
Vice President, Open Innovation, Kraft Foods

The value of the brand and protecting it as an intellectual asset globally is essential to success in generating revenue from a licensing program.

JOANNE BISCHMANN,
Vice President, Licensing and Special Events, Harley-Davidson

Success is measured by increased revenue generation coupled with increased awareness and positive association with the brand so that consumers want and demand it. They simply go hand in hand.

RUBY ZEFO,
Director, Trademarks and Brands, Intel

Want Your Brand Listed as a Top 100 Brand?

The big question for most branding professionals is: "How do I get my brands listed in the Top 100 lists?" There is no question in talking with the valuation experts that strong brands mean better long-term performance economically. But how do Interbrand and *BusinessWeek*, in their annual 100 Best Global Brands listings, calculate their valuation? How does Millward Brown calculate valuation in its top 100 list? Interbrand is one of the world's top brand consultancy firms with offices in 40 countries. Millward Brown likewise is one of the world's leading research companies, with offices in 50 countries, and works with 70 of the top 100 global brands. Do they value brands in the same way as the valuation experts?

Interbrand has a three-step approach to determine the 100 best global brands. First, they calculate how much of a company's total revenue or sales is directly related to a specific brand.

Second, they eliminate operating costs, taxes, and charges for the capital used to arrive at the total sales number, resulting in revenue generated by the intangible assets of the company. Interbrand then estimates the portion of that number attributed to other intangible assets such as patents, trade secrets, and management strengths to arrive at revenue generated by the brand number.

The final part of the analysis includes determining a net present value of future earnings to be generated by the brand by discounting that number against interest rates and overall risk profile. This means evaluating the strength of the intellectual property associated with the brand. How likely is the name or slogan to be diluted globally either by counterfeiting or by the weakness of the trademark? How likely is the product design and packaging to remain distinguished and unique? How long will the current ad campaign, music, or overall design remain powerful in the consumer mind? All of the things that you might think about in the creative process will be evaluated by Interbrand when determining the value of the most prominent brands.

The final result is a figure both *BusinessWeek* and Interbrand believe is closest to representing a brand's true economic worth.

A few other criteria worth noting for inclusion on the Interbrand list: The brand must be a consumer brand or market-facing brand, have publicly available financial data, and must demonstrate positive economic value.

Jez Frampton, CEO of Interbrand, is quoted on Interbrand's web site: "Understanding where we go and understanding change, the role of brands are more important than any other time before. CEO/Chief Marketing Officers are looking for inspiration in every corner of the world. . . . Understanding how it will create value in the future is more important than ever before and understanding how it might generate value in the future is critical."

Millward Brown has a similar calculation. They also have a three-step approach, which they tout as an economic or income-based approach similar to that used by the industry experts.

Step One: What portion of a company's earnings is generated under the banner of the brand? This provides for subtracting company operation or capital charges not related to the brand.

Step Two: How much of these branded earnings are generated due to the brand's close bond with its consumers? This is determined by understanding an analysis of country, market, and brand-specific consumer research that identifies brand contribution to consumer perceptions and behavior.

Step Three: What is the growth potential of the brand-driven earnings? This step focuses on the likelihood of continued growth of the brand by evaluating both financial projections and consumer data.

According to Millward Brown's 2009 report of the top 100 brands, in the year of global financial turmoil, when every key financial indicator plummeted, the value of the top 100 brands increased by 2 percent to $2 trillion. Brands remain among a company's most valuable assets. Strong brands have the power to create real and sustainable competitive advantage. They can drive revenue growth by ensuring higher demand and market share, help improve margins by commanding premium prices and better supplier terms, and reduce capital requirements by minimizing the costs of entry into new categories. Strong brands can also create differentiation that allows companies to overcome commoditization and reduce overall business risk.

According to both Interbrand and Millward Brown's top 100 brands lists, some of the top brands, in alphabetical order, include the following:

- Amazon
- American Express
- Apple
- BlackBerry
- BMW
- China Mobile
- Coca-Cola
- Disney
- General Electric
- Gillette
- Google
- H&M
- HP
- IBM
- ICBC
- Intel
- Louis Vuitton

(Continued)

(Continued)
- Marlboro
- McDonald's
- Mercedes-Benz
- Microsoft
- Nokia
- Oracle
- Pepsi
- SAP
- Samsung
- TESCO
- Toyota
- UPS
- Vodafone
- Walmart

Brands and the emotional connection they have to their consumer base can carry a company forward for decades, if not centuries. Once built, brands can produce huge returns on investment, allowing companies to maximize the use of their resources.

While the valuation team may be looking at cash flow, others involved in the creation of brand equity may be looking at other factors. Instead of measuring economic value, many in branding prefer to measure consumer behavior and attitudes that have an impact on the economic performance of brands. This follows very traditional market research models in quantifying consumer perceptions that drive buying behavior. According to the article from Interbrand, "Ad Agencies vs. Consultancies: Weighing the Difference" (2009), this may include levels of awareness, knowledge, familiarity, relevance, specific image attributes, purchase considerations, preference, satisfaction, and recommendation.

As a branding or innovation leader, how do you bridge the gap between what characterizes strong brand equity and a powerful brand with the formula used by a valuation professional when your company is looking to capitalize on its investment? And, even more to the point, how do you ensure that when you build a brand, you produce the greatest ROI?

In our research of top IP valuation professionals, one thing was clear. Regardless of the reason for the valuation, the key issue to each of them is what type of cash flow can be generated from the brand. So we thought it wise to look at the top global brands and identify what characteristics they all shared. Since we can assume that if these brands are on the Top 100 Brands list, they are each generating a certain amount of cash flow, what are the things that differentiate the top 100 brands from other brands?

We asked our panel of branding experts what they saw as the key characteristics of the most successful brands.

> Creating an emotional bond with consumers is one of the strongest ways for a brand to inspire loyalty. Consumers will pay a premium for a brand, or consistently choose it over another, if it stirs meaningful memories or feelings. A brand that can do this has the power to become instantly recognizable to not only its followers, but to those outside its usual consumer clique.
>
> KATHY SELKER,
> President, Northlich

> Powerful brands are constantly evolving to be relevant to their consumers. The really good ones (i.e. Virgin) broadly reach across product categories, always delivering on their promise to the consumer. Consumers want to identify with brands. They connect emotionally with brands whether they realize it or not.
>
> BILL THIEMANN,
> Executive Vice President, and
> BENTON SAUER,
> Vice President of Innovation, LPK

> A strong brand above all else will connect with the consumer in a powerful way. We evaluate all aspects of the consumer experiences from the look and feel of the product, to the experience in the retail or buying environment. At the top of our list in creating any campaign is to ensure that we connect to our consumer.
>
> KYLE McQUAID,
> Senior Vice President, J Walter Thompson

Then we asked a series of intellectual property lawyers the same question. What about these brands offers high intellectual property value?

The most powerful brands in the world are unique, arbitrary terms rather than descriptive ones. Coincidentally, those are also the ones that make the strongest trademarks.

GREGG MARRAZZO,
Vice President and Chief Counsel,
Intellectual Property and Global Marketing, Kimberly-Clark

Strong brands will be protected from multiple aspects of intellectual property and maintain the integrity of the brand at all levels with careful anticounterfeiting plans and protection plans in tandem with plans to capitalize globally on the brand.

NILS MONTAN,
Former Warner Bros. Chief Trademark Counsel,
Former President, International Trademark Association,
Former President, International AntiCounterfeiting Association

The strongest brands are those that are protected vigorously by their owners. They ensure that no new product lines or derivative brands dilute or distract from the core message and core belief that the brand conveys to its loyal followers. At Kodak, my primary goal is to ensure that nothing hurts our brand. Kodak stands for memories captured in the highest quality way. Whether it is a traditional camera, a digital camera, a home printer, the paper, the photograph, or some other new technology, the brand must be at the forefront of the marketing messages. We cannot tarnish or hurt our brand.

DAVID STIMSON,
Chief Trademark Counsel, Kodak, and
Former President of the International Trademark Association

Great brands are unique and distinctive. There are many components to what make a great brand, all of which can be protected. We look for the pillars of a brand—those foundational pieces that connect with the consumer—and then look for opportunities to create a sonic brand—one that ties in all senses of the experience—how it looks, how it sounds, what you feel, what you think.

JEROME MCDONNELL,
Senior Trademark Consultant, Interbrand

Although most trademark lawyers will tell you that coined, distinctive or completely made-up words are the most valuable—which is true—many times a descriptive word can also be powerful if the strategy behind it is focused on quickly penetrating a consumer base or in building off a parent brand. Sometimes the simpler, the better and the more focused it is, the better. What really matters is that the consumer understands what it is, why it has value, and who made it.

RUBY ZEFO,
Director, Trademarks and Brands, Intel

The most common similarity between what branding professionals and trademark lawyers think makes a great brand is that there are multiple components to a brand. There is not just one factor that makes it a success. For the branding professional, there are multiple layers that go into building the consumer experience, from how it looks and feels, to the way a campaign is targeted to touch a consumer's life at every level.

And from an intellectual property perspective, there are multiple tools that can protect all of the components of the product and the brand experience. The name, the slogan, the package design, the design of the product, the technical aspects of the product, the campaign, everything that touches the consumer experience—the more all of those aspects attain high intellectual property value, the greater and the longer that will translate into economic value.

To combine these two unique perspectives on what makes a great brand that can have long-term staying power means they both must be involved in the discussion from the outset. Asking the intellectual property specialist what makes a good trademark after hundreds of thousands of dollars have been spent developing the creative for the brand is too late. Likewise, simply saying "no" at the end of the process adds little value. An integrated team approach working toward a common goal is the solution to this problem.

Money is like an arm or a leg—use it or lose it.

HENRY FORD

Chapter Highlights

- Emerging companies in developing countries are seeking to boost their economic power globally by investing in brands. They are focused on how brands are valued in a global marketplace. To compete, established branding companies must also begin to consider how brands are valued.
- Brands remain one of the most powerful assets of most companies.
- The power of the brand on the company balance sheet can increase its borrowing power and the availability of capital. When competition for available capital is fierce, those companies with more powerful brands and intellectual assets on their balance sheet will obtain the necessary capital for continued growth.
- New accounting standards require annual valuation of brands and all intangible assets. If the brand loses market value, the company will have limited borrowing power. In the current economic climate, companies cannot afford to lose brand value.
- Strategically considering intellectual property early in the innovation or branding process simply makes good business sense. Otherwise, millions of dollars may be wasted on something with little long-term value or the company may be exposed to costly lawsuits. Thinking about it early costs the company less money and produces better results.
- Intellectual assets include brands, goodwill, patents, trademarks, trade secrets, copyrights, and other forms of source identification of a company's products and services.
- Valuation professionals will typically use an income approach, considering the likely continued cash flow or profits generated by a brand, reduced by any risk factors affecting the projected future revenue and profits of the brand.
- Brands can be diluted by obsolescence in the marketplace, a weak trademark that limits protection globally, counterfeiting, loss of faith and belief in the brand, competitive brands capturing market share, and overall limited intellectual property to ensure its sustainability.
- Interbrand, *BusinessWeek*, and Millward Brown also value brands each year, identifying the top 100 brands based upon

a three-pronged approach utilizing financial measures, but focusing on identifying the specific value generated to the company by the brand.

- Branding professionals and intellectual property specialists alike find that there are many components to what makes a good brand, and that it is only when they combine in that rare form that value is created. Multidisciplinary teams are needed in the current economic climate to fully tap into the power of the brand on a long-term basis.

3

Designing in IP

Now that we have captured your attention as to why it is important in developing branding campaigns to consider intellectual property, we begin by stating the obvious.

We have consistently found in our research that intellectual property is generally not considered at the outset of creating a branding or marketing campaign. Occasionally it may be considered midstream, but it is most often considered at the end of the creative process as a "clearance" by legal rather than as a strategic advantage.

For clarification, in this book the term *brand* or *branding* defines all aspects of messaging used to build or reinforce the power of the brand. When we suggest designing IP into a branding campaign, it means into the creative process used to create any messaging, programs, or campaigns related to the consumer belief in the brand, whether it is a new or existing brand.

> We have worked hard to create a culture where intellectual property strategy is a part of the overall business thinking. It is easy for a company to spend hundreds of thousands of dollars on a branding campaign only to find it can't be protected or at least not to the extent desired. At Yahoo! we turn that process on its head and build in a team of professionals who understand that we are a company of intellectual assets and that there must be a clear strategy behind everything we do.
>
> J. SCOTT EVANS,
> Senior Legal Director,
> Global Brands and Trademarks, Yahoo!

Intellectual property strategy should be part of the brand strategy from the outset. What we outline here is to help the creative team recognize that all of what you do can be protected and bolster the value of your work to the company. We understand and believe that branding professionals should be focused on what they do best and that having lawyers in the room may not necessarily be helpful in the creative process. However, a new professional, a Brand Maestro, must emerge to help bridge this important gap and intersect at the right times. This chapter will provide practical tips for understanding where the intellectual property value comes from in what you are already doing in building a branding campaign. Elements of branding can be protected by patents, trademarks, trade dress, trade secrets, and copyright. For any lawyers or technical specialists reading this chapter, we do not intend this to be a comprehensive case law or statutory review, but rather an overview of what basic elements should be considered when creating a brand campaign.

There are several basic components of intellectual property that will be discussed.

According to the World Intellectual Property Organization, a patent has the following features:

Protects	Useful, new, and nonobvious processes and products.
Lasts	20 years from the filing date of the application for a utility patent and 14 years from the date of registration for a design patent.
Scope	Excludes others from making, using, selling, offering, or importing the patented invention.
Caveat	In the United States, must file within one year from first date of public use.

The U.S. Copyright Office explains that copyright has the following features:

Protects	Works of authorship including writings, books, papers, photographs, music, art, movies, commercials, recordings, software, or other ideas reduced to tangible written form.

(Continued)

Lasts   In the United States, life of author plus 70 years or 95 years for work made for hire.

Scope   Prevents others from reproducing or distributing copies, preparing derivative works, performing or displaying the work publicly, or transmitting it.

Caveat   While filing is not needed, it increases the need for protection and ability to seek remedies in court. Additionally, to ensure global protection under the Berne Convention, filing in the United States is required.

The U.S. Patent and Trademark Office notes that trademarks and trade dress have the following features:

Protects   Words, personal names, letters, numerals, figurative elements, combinations of colors, sounds, symbols, distinctive designs, other devices used to distinguish goods and services (i.e., your brand name, logo, and tagline).

Lasts   In the United States, as long as you use it in the marketplace.

Scope   Excludes others from using the mark to cause a likelihood of confusion to the consumer and to prevent others from diluting the mark.

Caveat   You must file in the correct product categories and you must constantly monitor and police usage to maintain the value of the trademark in order to obtain the protection needed to stop others from using it.

For trade secrets, the U.S. Patent and Trademark Office explains that they have the following features:

Protects   An idea, process, formula, recipe, know-how, technology, ingredient, or other aspect of how a product or service is created or delivered that is kept secret.

Lasts   As long as you take measures to keep it a secret.

Scope   Prevents others from disclosing, using, or acquiring it by dishonest means.

Caveat   You must use nondisclosure agreements and document the measures you take to keep it a secret.

Branding involves a number of components. At its core, branding must include:

- Clear name/word identity for each aspect of the product/service that is unique and distinctive.
- Clear visual/design identity for each aspect of the product/service.
- Strong, focused messaging to convey and build power behind the name and build a loyal, emotional connection with the consumer.
- Clear understanding of the message to be conveyed to the target audience so that the brand accomplishes the objective of building consumer confidence in the product or service.
- Continuous reinforcement through messaging. Whether the message is received on a mobile device, on a computer, in the news, in print or television campaigns, in a movie, while traveling, in the retail location—wherever a message is heard it must continuously reinforce the consumer's belief in the promise of the brand.

A few of our experts have weighed in on other components to consider.

If you know where your brand has adjacencies and growth opportunities, you can make better decisions in the development process. Understand how what you are developing can be protected and build the wall of protection high enough to maximize protecting your brands and products from being knocked-off by others—then you have something far more valuable. It's not just about playing defense, it's about playing offense.

JEFF WEEDMAN,
Vice President, Global Business
Development, Procter & Gamble

A great brand will be a pillar of the company and serve as a distinctive essence of what the company or product means to the consumer.

JEROME McDONNELL,
Senior Trademark Consultant, Interbrand

Yahoo!'s brand is our most powerful asset. A trademark is not just a rubber stamp. It is a critical part of the brand itself. We get that at Yahoo!

> J. SCOTT EVANS,
> Senior Legal Director,
> Global Brands and Trademarks, Yahoo!

A great brand will be consistent and dependable to its loyal consumer, always delivering or exceeding expectations. The greatest brands will always strive for the highest quality, never cutting corners, and every message in marketing and advertising will reinforce that promise. For the consumer, a great brand is one that he or she would choose over any competitor.

> BOB WEHLING,
> Former Global Marketing Officer, Procter & Gamble

The Creative Process

To illustrate how to intersect intellectual property thinking into the creative process, let's assume that we are working on an innovative new product tied to a service for a large company, ready to launch either a new brand or a series of sub-brands. There are a series of steps that need to take place.

- Identify what needs to be branded and why.
- Determine if an existing brand may better support this new product, service, or idea. Will the existing brand protection allow global expansion into this product category? Is there any exposure to risk of infringement by expanding the brand? How much will it cost to create and protect a new brand versus build off an existing one?
- Identify the target market for each component of the product/service.
- Define the market in detail to understand the consumer lifestyle; build a profile of your consumer.
- Identify the market structure, opinion leaders, and influencers.
- Identify competitors and competitors' brands and understand how and why consumers might choose them over yours.

- Identify the objective for the brand.
- Define what the brand experience should be:
  - What should it look and feel like, and what should it sound like?
  - What problem does this solve?
  - What need does it serve?
  - What other brands will this work with or against?
  - What is the value of the brand?
  - If the brand were a person, how would you describe it?
  - Does it avoid pain, reduce pain, or provide pleasure?
  - What are the features, advantages, and benefits?
  - What stories can be told about the brand?
- Develop brand and campaign ideas through a creative process of researching and understanding the market and understanding objectives. This is a process unto itself and there are many tools and tips for developing good ideas. While we want to remain focused on intellectual property thinking, there is much written and much that could be discussed on the process of generating good ideas for the brand and its campaign to connect with consumers. Generate a minimum of 3–5 ideas.
- Search the brand names for trademarkability and potential infringement on other marks, exploring maximum exploitation globally and valuation principles in the process (i.e., not just is it available, but is it strong as a trademark?). Consider all aspects of the potential campaign and identify what can be protected and what might be used to bolster the valuation of the campaign. Are there colors, sounds, looks, feels to the overall consumer experience? Could there be? Is there a unique design to any component of the product or the packaging? How can we add something new and different that is so distinctive that it can only be associated with this product? What aspects can be protected? How can we improve the intellectual property value of our 3–5 core ideas? Which one will provide the most return on investment as an intellectual asset of the company? These questions must be asked at this time in order to have maximum impact.
  - There is an important distinction to make at this step. This analysis is about risk and exploitation.

- Risk—will using this name expose us in any way to potential infringement action throughout the globe? What is the cost benefit analysis of that risk?
- Exploitation—is this strong enough that we can stop others from using it? *Many times, it may be a weak mark that can be used without risk, but that means anyone can use it and it will be difficult and costly to stop them.*

- Continue the process until one to three brands with clear and high intellectual property value have been created.
- Conduct appropriate market or other research test of the brands to select the final brand.
- Continue the process until market and IP research bring consistent results.
- Develop implementation of the branding plan at all levels of the company.
- Review the entire campaign to ensure that no aspects will infringe on other rights and that it is compliant with all FTC guidelines. Is everything the truth? Can you prove it? This is a comprehensive search that involves verification that no copyright, trademark, rights of privacy or publicity or other rights have been or could be perceived to infringe on the rights of any third party, as well as to ensure that all claims of the ad are true and can be supported.
- Apply for the appropriate intellectual property protection and develop a plan to police and protect. This means monitoring worldwide use of the intellectual property and taking steps to stop infringers.
- All separable elements of the identity should be researched for availability and protected to the fullest extent available. A complete set of branding standards should be prepared for the company to utilize in ensuring consistency in building the power of the brand.
- The implementation of these standards should be policed both inside and outside of your company. Many companies maintain their own inspectors across the world ensuring compliance to brand identity standards and detecting infringements.

In order to legally protect a trademark, it should be registered in the country in which it is used, and it should be identified as a pending or registered trademark to give notice of the intended protection. In the United States, the U.S. Patent and Trademark Office (USPTO) is the government agency responsible for administration of trademarks.

One of the most important fundamentals to consider when building a brand and understanding how the creative work intersects with intellectual property is to remember that generally trademark law gives legal protection to the name or brand that stands out so brightly that a consumer would only identify it with a particular company.

The overarching goal of the USPTO is to ensure that consumers are not confused. The USPTO recognizes that companies work hard to build the goodwill and reputation associated with their products or services and wants to provide protection for consumers so that they do not mistakenly buy a product thinking it is of a certain quality only to find out it is a knock-off. This is why there is exclusivity for names within certain categories, and when there are names within other categories, the trademark office analyzes how likely a consumer is to be confused when determining whether to issue the trademark.

Based upon that overarching goal, the general questions considered by a trademark examining attorney in analyzing whether to allow a trademark to become a registered trademark are as follows:

- Is anyone else using this mark in a similar classification?
- If so, would a consumer be confused as to the origin of the product or service?
- Is the name merely descriptive of the product such that it should not be given trademark protection?
- Is the name generic such that it should not be given trademark protection?
- Is it unique and distinctive enough to be provided protection?

Creative teams also want to ensure that the brand stands out from the crowd. They work to ensure that their consumer would not confuse their brand with anyone else's. The goals are the same: Stand out from the crowd—be noticed—be distinctive—be unique.

There are a few key general legal considerations to keep in mind when developing a brand.

- The brand should provide a clear legal path to obtain intellectual property protection (globally) and ensure it does not infringe on any other intellectual property rights. This requires analysis and should be carefully considered at the beginning of the process.
- Without clear federal and international intellectual property clearance and protection, any brand developed may have roadblocks to use in the marketplace, as well as limited value to the corporation, diminishing the return on investment.
- There must be a branding policy to ensure all uses of the brand by the company in all materials and messaging are consistent to build the power of the brand and reinforce the legal rights afforded to it.
- Unique, fanciful, made-up terms that are not generally used to define the product or service being provided will have the greatest value in creating intellectual property. If the name is too descriptive, not only will you not be able to protect it, but anyone can use it as well, meaning you will not have exclusivity in the name and the value is diminished. If it is generic, it has no value.
- Use of a traditional term being applied in a new manner can also be very powerful, such as Apple for computers.
- A logo design that is unique and new will have tremendous power (for example, the Nike swoosh).
- There should be no other trademarks that are similar (i.e., in sound, words, design) in similar classifications of product categories. There are literally millions of trademarks in the USPTO and even more throughout the world in hundreds of classifications of products or services. Selecting something without widespread use will have more value. Yes, it's often harder creatively, but then it has that much more value.
- The intended use of the mark must not compete or potentially confuse consumers with any other registered or pending trademark. Because of the vast number of trademarks already registered, it is essential to be running searches contemporaneously with the branding process to ensure the ability to protect the mark. This includes a detailed search of the USPTO database, as well as extensive Internet searches for any potential marks that might create confusion for the consumer base. The primary distinction is whether a potential

consumer might be confused as to the origin of the product or service.

- The more differentiated the mark is, the more value it has legally.
- If it merely describes the product or service or is generic, it cannot be protected. This is an important distinction, as more readily the USPTO is rejecting marks on this basis. With the overpopulation of brands and trademarks since electronic applications became available, this scrutiny has become a barrier of entry for many trademarks.
- The trademark application process typically takes 12–18 months, and in the meantime, we need to properly identify our trademark as a pending trademark with the symbol ™ and then later, upon registration, the symbol ®.
- Colors can be trademarked if they are unique to the product or service and utilized in a meaningful and distinctive manner (i.e., if the color for the product is indicative of the product itself). Consider the following:
  - Use of the color yellow for Post-it notes
  - Kodak's yellow color scheme on its logo and product packaging
  - Pink for insulation by Owens Corning
  - Use of the color blue for the Tiffany box
- Sounds can be trademarked:
  - Use of the unique tones for Intel
  - NBC's chimes
  - Use of the yodel for Yahoo!
- Product and packaging designs can be trademarked as a form of trade dress.
  - The Coca-Cola bottle
  - Herman Miller chairs
  - Hermes bags
- Trademarks can be applied as an intent to use mark or as an in use mark. Under either application, eventually the marketing materials used must actually contain the trademark as applied for and not one that has evolved into some variation. Any change in the trademark in any way will require a new application.
- Once the trademark is obtained and a brand is being developed, regular monitoring to ensure that the mark is not infringed upon by others is essential. All too often, valuable

brands are created and then diluted because the trademark holder does not enforce the rights. Best practices in monitoring include weekly review of the *Official Gazette* in order to oppose any marks published for opposition and pending registration that may create confusion or dilute your trademark. Also, regular Google searches to ascertain any other use of the brand is essential. This can be done at a grassroots level internally on a cost-effective basis, or a more formal monitoring program can be put in place with global searching companies.

- Generally, the more differentiated the identity, the easier it is to protect from infringement. Competitors will often pick up on elements of the look and feel of the brand leader. They must be confronted; otherwise the trademark is lost as a valuable piece of intellectual property and, more importantly, the clarity of your identity (a key piece of communication between your brand and your consumers) becomes diluted in confounding "noise" from other brands.

To further explore how to design thinking about intellectual property into the creative process, let's explore each aspect of a branding campaign and detail what could be protected.

Product Packaging and Product Design

The product design as well as the product packaging can be protected by trademark, trade dress, design patents, and sometimes, copyright law so long as they meet the right criteria, are protected, and are enforced (all important conditions to protection).

Consider some of the great success stories, all of which have been afforded trademark protection under the expanding rules that allow unique product shapes, colors, and scents:

- Christian Louboutin shoes' unique red sole
- The Hermes distinctive Birkin bag
- Apple's iPod design
- Herman Miller furniture design
- Yamaha Motor Corporation's unique arc of the water flowing from its watercraft
- Ferrari product design

Each of these products can be protected by design patents and/ or trademark/trade dress law. The key to success in protection as an intellectual asset is that their owners invest marketing budgets in building an association in the consumer's mind that these distinctive and nonfunctional features are unique only to their product line. This type of evidence is necessary to obtain protection of product and package designs for certain forms of trademark protection. Consider the various forms of protecting a product package or product design.

Design patents have a life of 14 years from the date of issuance, whereas trademarks can last forever, so long as they continue to be used and protected. Design patents can be issued for new, original, and ornamental design for an article of manufacture. A design patent protects only the appearance of the article and not its structural or utilitarian features. It can be very useful in conjunction with trademark law to ensure exclusivity in the design, particularly if it may take time to invest in the consumer connection to the design in order to be afforded trademark protection. For example, many companies may apply for a design patent to protect the design itself, then invest in marketing and advertising to create an iconic consumer connection to that design, and then, armed with that information, apply for the trademark. The trademark then lasts forever and continues to provide protection when the design patent expires. The design patent, however, was useful by providing that initial protection to box out competitors in the early phases while consumer identification was still being developed.

A subset of trademark law known as trade dress can protect the unique colors and designs of the package. The key to the registration of any trademark/trade dress is that it cannot be in use by another registrant in the same or similar product classifications. This is an important point—you can only register in product categories that you are using or intend to use within a reasonable time period. Companies can use it in other nonrelated product categories. The key is that it cannot cause potential confusion to consumers as to the source or origin of the product. Additionally, for the nontraditional trademark, such as design, sounds, colors, and smells, it must be proven to be nonfunctional and distinctive. This will frequently require proof by the company that there is meaning associated with the distinctive characteristic to the extent that it is widely known. Fender Guitars recently lost its bid for protection of its design because it was found to be too common or functional and not distinctive of the product as a brand. However, Christian Louboutin was able to obtain protection for its very distinctive red sole because it is clearly nonfunctional and a source indicator.

Copyright law can protect any specific unique artistic renderings or designs that adorn the packaging—anything that would be considered artwork can be copyrighted. Copyright protection will last the life of the artist plus 70 years if by an individual, or 95 years if it is work-for-hire (i.e., a company pays someone to provide the creative). The basic element is that it is an original work of authorship in tangible form that can include literary works, musical works, dramatic works, choreography, pictorial, graphic or sculptures, motion pictures and audiovisual works, sound recordings, and architectural works. If a product has a unique artistic rendering as part of its packaging, such as the Kleenex box designs—meaning the art on the box—then it also can be protected by copyright law.

Our experts comment on the power of product design and packaging:

> Packaging is equally as powerful as any other form of marketing and particularly has enduring intellectual property value. I always advise considering how we are packaging our products, how we are using our trademark colors, and reinforcing what that means to our consumers.
>
> DAVID STIMSON,
> Chief Trademark Counsel, Kodak, and
> Former President, International Trademark Association

> The graphics on the box are protected by the copyright law and the dispensing feature is protected by the patent statute. Of course, it all ties back to our brand, Kleenex, which is a trademark we rigorously enforce around the globe. In terms of creating economic value in a new product, this was a tremendous success.
>
> GREGG MARRAZZO,
> Vice President and Chief Counsel,
> Intellectual Property and Global Marketing, Kimberly-Clark

Every expression leaves an impression. Make every impression count.

BENTON SAUER,
Vice President of Innovation, LPK

Consumer packaging is one of the most important aspects of a brand. This is the first moment a consumer interacts with the product.

It must do many things. It must seamlessly weave into the manufacturing process without error.

It must be environmentally friendly.

It must be cost effective.

It must be functional (i.e., all Starbucks cups use the same size lid—that's not an accident).

It must be as powerful to the consumer as the product itself is.

It must be iconic and define the product to the consumer.

CRAIG VOGEL,
Associate Dean, Design, Architecture,
Art and Planning, University of Cincinnati

As you develop your product designs and package designs, consider a few common questions about how to protect your product design and packaging.

- *Do I need to register trade dress?*

    Some aspects of trade dress can be registered as a trademark. In fact, one of the most famous trade dress cases, concerning a Mexican restaurant, was not about a registered mark of any kind, but rather the unique décor of a restaurant that was determined to be so unique and not functional that it could only belong to Two Pesos. This landmark case, *Two Pesos, Inc. v. Taco Caba, Inc.*, 112 S. Ct. 2753 (1992), paved the way for restaurateurs and retailers to evaluate the very look and feel of their store as intellectual property to stop imitators from infringing on their investment.

    Registration can bolster your ability to prevent others from imitating your product or service. In another landmark case, *Qualitex Co. v. Jacobson Products Co.*, No. 93-1577 (US March 28, 1995), it was determined that a color, if used in a nonfunctional and distinctive manner identifying it with the maker of the goods, could be a registered trademark. In this instance, Qualitex was able to stop its competitors from using its trademark green color on dry cleaning pads. The U.S. Trademark Office now directly permits the registration of a color if it meets the requirements of a trademark.

- *How do I protect my product designs?*

  If your product design itself is so unique that it can only be recognized as belonging to your company and it is not merely functional, then you may be able to protect it as a registered trademark design, also known as trade dress. Product designs can be a bit tricky, though. Passing the mark off as nonfunctional is not easy. A few examples of those who made it include:
  - Herman Miller
  - Ferrari
  - Apple
  - *Time* magazine cover
  - Fotomat building shape
  - White Castle building

  The design and format of magazine covers, the look of a greeting card line, the combination of features on a briefcase, and the layout of a point-of-sale display have all been held to be trade dress.

  The two basic elements to obtain protection:
  - The uniqueness of the design creates an instant connection as a source indicator of your company. Meaning, if you see the shape of a Ferrari, you don't confuse it with a Ford. Or, a Herman Miller chair is so distinctively Herman Miller that its source would not be confusing as being Thomasville.
  - The design must be nonfunctional.

- *How do I protect my product packages?*

  Unique product packages are one of the most cost-effective ways to build a powerful brand and differentiate yourself from competitors. Trade dress law allows you to prevent others from copying your unique product package designs. The classic example is the Coca-Cola bottle. This timeless shape differentiates Coca-Cola from all of its competitors and has withstood the test of time. The key is to remind your creative team that the product must go beyond functionality. For example, many product packages have a trademark design as part of the package, but the package itself is merely functional (i.e., a box or a bottle). To rise to the next level, working with your creative team to create something that goes beyond functionality can produce an iconic, protectable design that can last forever.

- *Can fashion designs be protected by trade dress law?*

While trade dress law has been expanding its protection in the United States to include product packaging and designs of products themselves, such as furniture or cars, it has not yet extended to fashion designs. Largely unprotected by U.S. law, fashion designers have long suffered from the inevitable copying of their designs. No sooner do the designers show their collection for the next season than less costly manufacturers have largely stolen the look, color, and feel of the collection to sell at bargain prices. Copyright law does not protect the design, because it is determined to be merely utilitarian. As it has been argued, the design is for the purpose of creating clothing to be worn, rather than as a unique individual piece of art or original work. While designers will surely argue the opposite, this has long been the standard in the United States, despite the protection afforded by other more fashion-friendly countries such as France.

It raises an interesting question, however. If the look or design is so unique and unchanging or unwavering that it could only be associated with a specific designer, that person could apply for a design mark to protect the design. From a practical perspective, this may not make economic sense. Most designers make money by bringing the latest designs each season. It takes longer than that to acquire secondary meaning and thus they would never meet the two-pronged test for trade dress. If, however, a designer developed an iconic-like piece that would withstand changing fashion climates, he or she could invoke this protection. For example, the classic Burberry pattern is a registered trademark.

- *Should I obtain both a design patent and a trademark for my product or package design?*

Yes, a design patent will provide important initial protection for a unique package design, allowing for time to invest in creating a consumer connection to the design. Once consumers widely know that the distinctive design is uniquely yours, then you will have the necessary evidence to apply for trademark protection. Trademark protection will then last forever.

- *What aspect of a product or package design can be copyrighted?*

Copyrights can provide additional protection if you create unique and original artwork or designs in the product packaging, such as what Kleenex did on its boxes. Then the art can be protected along with the package design itself. Copyright requires original writing or art created in tangible form. It will last the life of the creator plus 70 years or 95 years for a work-for hire. A work-for-hire is generally any work created that is paid for by someone else and assigned over for that fee.

Registration is always recommended to ensure maximum protection. Registration is done through the Library of Congress by submitting an application, a sample, and a filing fee of $35. Copyright notifications should be placed on the materials: Copyright followed by date and name or © followed by date and name.

Name and Logo Design

Branding companies such as Interbrand emerged in the early 1970s when a brand was thought of primarily as a name and a logo. While the name and logo design continue to be a core part of any brand, it is widely recognized to be only one piece of a complete brand campaign. It is often, however, the foundation that builds the power of the brand experience. As you create new names or logos for brands or sub-brands, consider what makes it powerful and what can be used to increase its value. Remember, fundamentally, a name and logo is about creating something so that consumers know what they are buying—delivering on a promise. The more unique and distinctive that is, creatively and as intellectual property, the more value it has as a brand.

As discussed in Chapter 2, Interbrand and Millward Brown annually define the best brands in the world primarily based upon market value. From the creative and intellectual property perspective, there are several elements that will make a brand stand out and be powerful.

- *What are the characteristics of a strong trademark or logo?*

  A strong trademark or logo will be unique, distinctive, arbitrary, or fanciful. This means you will have to do more and spend more to market it to consumers. It doesn't simply describe what the product is, so you will have to educate the consumer on a nondescriptive mark. Many companies will weigh the cost of investing in a unique or arbitrary mark rather than a descriptive one. However, the distinctive and unique mark will have significantly more power on a long-term basis from both a branding and an intellectual property perspective, likely producing greater long-term return on investment. It will also be easier to stop others from infringing on a unique trademark versus a descriptive one. The IP strategists and trademark lawyers we talked to all explained that those descriptive marks that seem so easy to use usually can't be owned by a company and can be copied by others.

  Additionally, no other company can be using a mark that is similar in the same product categories or that would confuse consumers.

  Likewise, a strong logo will be iconic in nature, not simply a mere reflection of what the product is. For example, a shoe company's logo that has a shoe in it would not be a distinctive logo. Unique designs and colors are more powerful as a trademark. While the requirement is simply that there is not another design like it in the same categories and it is not likely to cause confusion, the more unique and distinctive, the greater impact it will have in the long term.

- *How do I protect it globally?*

  This is becoming an increasingly important question. If the trademark is intended for global exploitation, a full research and analysis of any competitive or similar brands worldwide must be conducted to determine if it can be protected in all of the intended countries. The trademark must then be registered in all countries in which you intend to exploit the mark. While organizations like the International Trademark Association continue to work toward consistency in trademark laws and enforcement, differences do exist and careful counsel on these issues is required.

- *How long does the trademark last?*

  The trademark will last as long as you continue to use it in the marketplace. Essentially, a trademark can last forever. If you cease using it in the marketplace, however, then it is subject to cancellation or abandonment, meaning it becomes open for anyone else to take it and use it. This is particularly important for large companies that built a brand but do not continue to exploit it. If they simply stop using it, then they can't maintain it as a trademark.

- *What do I have to do to maintain the trademark?*

  In addition to certain filings required with the U.S. Patent and Trademark Office and in other administrative offices globally, to ensure that a mark retains its status and power, it must be protected. If you simply allow others to infringe and use your mark without enforcing it, then it can later be canceled for failure to protect and maintain. A strong anticounterfeiting and dilution program is not just good for business from a branding perspective, but important to ensure that the intellectual property value is not diminished.

- *What can bolster the value of a brand?*

  A powerful technique is to build upon a parent brand and create a series of sub-brands that bolster the value and exclusivity of that brand. A great example is McDonald's, which created a whole line of products that are each afforded its own trademark protection: Egg McMuffin, Big Mac, McNuggets, and so on. Likewise, Apple created its series of i-products: iPod, iPhone, iMac.

One of my key concerns in any new marketing initiative is to ensure that we continue to build on the power of the brand and in no way dilute the long-standing value we have in the Kodak brand. Kodak means memories, quality, and reliability, regardless of what the product might be. Whenever we are looking to create a sub-brand, I ask, why is this needed? Will our master Kodak brand do the trick rather than investing in something new?

DAVID STIMSON,
Chief Trademark Counsel, Kodak, and
Former President, International Trademark Association

I absolutely believe that frequently building off the core brand is smarter than creating new brands. The cost to protect a brand in 50–60 jurisdictions is staggering and often simply impossible. All new ideas don't have to have a new name. We have moved toward a philosophy of branding everything we do under Yahoo! rather than fragmenting our company into many different brands. We consider our company a "branded house" rather than a "house of brands." This becomes more efficient for us to manage on a global basis and allows us to fully capitalize on the power of that brand.

J. Scott Evans,
Senior Legal Director,
Global Brands and Trademarks, Yahoo!

We were one of the first companies to really brand something not directly sold to consumers. Intel Inside was a critical branding effort. Most of our sales are to other product companies who buy Intel products to put inside a computer or other device. The Intel Inside campaign reached out to consumers so that consumers were looking for products with Intel Inside. I think the key trend now is to simplify everything so consumers can figure out what they need quickly.

Ruby Zefo,
Director, Trademarks and Brands, Intel

Campaign and Connection to the Consumer

As the product design, package design, name, and logo all come together in the creative process, the next phase is to build a comprehensive campaign to connect to the consumer. This may include many aspects of interactive, mobile, print, television, movie placement, sponsorship, radio, direct mail, and other media for connecting to and reaching the consumer. Inevitably, certain aspects of that campaign can be protected to ensure that others cannot easily copy or mimic and capitalize on the goodwill created from your creative energies. Many times, the campaign can help to bolster a mark that is merely descriptive.

For example, Overstock.com (a descriptive mark; it describes that the company sells overstock items) evolved into a powerful brand through its marketing campaign. Overstock unveiled a national marketing and branding campaign that made Overstock worth over $1 billion. "Look for the O" created one of the best "stores" on the Web. According to Overstock.com, in 1999, the company had $1.8 million in sales; after new branding in late 2004, revenues rose to nearly $500 million.

Nearly all aspects of a campaign can be protected. Consider various components that might be used in a campaign.

Sounds and Music

So often, outrageous amounts of money are paid to license the rights to preexisting well-known music. While at times the value proposition of capturing existing emotions and beliefs associated with music is valuable, the ability to create new and powerful music that connects with the consumer and that can become a hallmark of the product/company is overlooked. Not only can it be more powerful creatively, but it can also be owned by the company through the copyright protection of the music. Rather than simply go to an existing portfolio of music, consider creating a contest and tapping into the vast talent of unknown musicians who would jump at the chance to write something of importance. Any such contest, of course, should be accompanied by contest rules clearly stating that the company owns the copyright to whatever music is submitted. Thinking outside the box and creating new music that resonates with your consumer base provides higher return on investment. Specific sounds that are unique and distinctive can be trademarked, as stated above, and original music or jingles can be copyrighted.

Additionally, unique sounds can be trademarked in a campaign. For example, the Twentieth Century Fox drumroll, Pillsbury Doughboy's giggle, Nokia default ringtone, NBC chimes, and MGM lion roar are all registered U.S. trademarks.

Copy

The copy written for print ads can be copyrighted. Likewise, commercials can be copyrighted to ensure that the various distinctive aspects of the print and audiovisual ad campaigns are exclusive. Specific slogans or taglines that are created can often be protected by trademark law, which will have a longer life cycle.

Art and Characters

Additionally, if unique art is used for a print ad or in a commercial or a unique character is created, such as Tony the Tiger or Mr. Clean, the character can not only be trademarked, but may also be copyrighted as an artistic rendering. Characters prove to be iconic in nature often more easily than a for-hire spokesperson. Additionally, characters generally do what they are told and the companies that create them don't have to worry about the spokesperson having a breakdown or saying and doing things to tarnish the company's image. Characters are an often overlooked source of iconic spokespeople for a brand that can last forever.

General Marketing Themes

While ideas alone are not protected, as soon as they are fixed in some tangible form, as outlined in this chapter, they can be protected.

The overall look, feel, and theme of your campaign can be protected through the various sources outlined here. To maximize protection, it's important to identify what is truly unique and different and then determine how it is fixed in tangible form and what elements of IP protection can be used to ensure it is owned by the company.

Chefs and Signature Dishes

The name of the chef can be protected, but it is essential that the name, logo, and marketing materials are trademarked and, more importantly, that the appropriate license agreement is in place with the chef. The chef will have the right to use his or her name in any future endeavors, absent some type of agreement in place. Additionally, a signature dish can be protected if it is given a unique and nondescriptive name. As for the recipe itself, it must be protected by trade secret protection. Nothing has indicated that a recipe for a signature dish will rise to the level of protection by the trademark.

However, the unique shape of a food can be protected. For example, Pepperidge Farm's Goldfish have successfully precluded competitors from using a similar confusing shape of a gold fish for cheese crackers.

Avoiding Liability

A final important note for the creative team when developing a campaign: A risk analysis must be performed to ensure that nothing in the campaign will violate the rights of third parties nor any requirements of the FTC. This includes consideration of rights of privacy, publicity, trademark, copyright, and other third-party rights. This is not a simple matter. With the continued and rapid development of new technologies and the cost of lawsuits continually increasing, the potential exposure to risk and potential cost of a lawsuit for infringing must be carefully considered and a cost-benefit analysis performed. See the following section on FTC guidelines for more details. It may be determined that a calculated risk is important or that the benefit outweighs the risk, but those decisions should be made as informed decisions rather than as an unexpected negative response to a campaign. For example, Apple did not own the iPhone mark. Cisco had applied for a mark, but had not begun to use it in the marketplace. Apple likely made a calculated decision that the benefit outweighed the risk. The risk paid off. Apple settled the matter with Cisco and now owns the trademark for iPhone.

FTC Guidelines

The Federal Trade Commission governs advertising in the United States. Here are a few important points to keep in mind in building ad campaigns that can lead to liability if not addressed. For more detailed information, go to ftc.gov. They have many easy to read and useful guidebooks for professionals with important information about the regulations governing all advertising in the United States.

Disclaimers must be clear and conspicuous. Yes, this means small type that can't be read is a problem.

Demonstrations must show how the product will perform under normal use.

Refunds must be made to dissatisfied consumers if you promise to make them.

Advertising directed to children has specific requirements. The Children's Advertising Review Unit (CARU) of the Council of the Better Business Bureau has specific guidelines for children's advertising.

The Children's Online Privacy Protection Act provides very specific guidelines for online promotion to children. Any web site directed to children under 13 years old or general sites that know they are collecting information from children must obtain a parent's permission before collecting that information. More information can be found at http://www.ftc.gov/privacy/privacyinitiatives/childrens.html.

Any advertising of credit terms must specifically follow the truth in lending act.

Any use of the words "free" or "buy one, get one" has specific requirements that must be followed.

All products delivered by mail must be capable of being delivered within 30 days or you must expressly state the time frame for delivery.

Negative option offers, such as programs that invite you to enroll in a program after a free trial and continue your monthly subscription unless you opt out, have very specific rules to describe the opt-out option.

All 900-number calls must disclose the rates of the call.

Testimonials or endorsements must reflect the typical experience of the consumer and must be substantiated.

Use of the word "guaranteed" means you must be willing to give a full refund for any reason.

Use of the term "Made in the USA" means the product must be all or virtually all made in the United States.

Bottom line: *always tell the truth.*

A few comments from our thought leaders on the campaign and the value of incorporating multidisciplinary thinking into the strategic process:

> If we could be brought in earlier and work with the marketing professionals internally as well as have the opportunity to brief the advertising agencies, we could have a much richer outcome.
>
> GREGG MARRAZZO,
> Vice President and Chief Counsel,
> Intellectual Property and Global Marketing, Kimberly-Clark

Sound is absolutely an important part of our mark. In fact, we recently held contests for the Yahoo! Yodel, involving our consumer base in our marketing campaign, as well as creating something that will have long-term trademark value for us.

J. Scott Evans,
Senior Legal Director,
Global Brands and Trademarks, Yahoo!

At the heart of our process is collaboration. We want the right stimulus, which means we need the right people from various disciplines for the formation of good ideas.

Bill Thiemann,
Executive Vice President, and
Benton Sauer,
Vice President of Innovation, LPK

Culture

The final component of an overall product launch and campaign is the culture and the way in which the product is sold. Depending upon the type of product, it may range from the design and layout of a store and retail environment, the slogans used to sell the product, or operations guides that provide detailed training for the employees who deliver the services. The culture of how your store or restaurant associates look and behave can have some aspects of intellectual property protection. There are some companies widely known for their unparalleled consumer experience; for example, Ritz-Carlton, Four Seasons, Nordstrom, Disney, Tiffany. For these companies, the most important component of their competitive advantage does not need intellectual property protection as it is something that takes leadership to implement and create—flawless execution of superior consumer experience and service. The one thing that has the greatest value of all is employee loyalty to the ideals of the company. Some aspects of what it takes to create that culture, though, can be protected. For example:

- The décor can be protected by trade dress law.
- Training and operations methods can be protected by trade secret law.

- The logo of the company that is trademarked can be proudly showcased on name badges, uniforms, or other distinctive attire and accessories.
- Levels of service or status within the company can be protected under trade secret law if they are maintained as confidential within the culture of the organization.

The Retail Environment

Trade dress can also protect the actual physical layout and unique design of a restaurant, retail, or other environment so long as it rises to the level of being nonfunctional and uniquely distinctive. As you consider the design and layout of a specific section of a retail environment, consider that a unique and fanciful design that is not functional may be something that can not only be protected, but become a hallmark of the product line.

Is it so unique and distinctive that if you walked into the store, you would know it was your store versus any other competitor? What about it provides that unique distinction? Can you prove that there is secondary meaning associated with the layout and design of your store in order to apply for protection? Example of restaurants include Fuddruckers, T.G.I. Friday's, Hooters—note the characteristics that take it to the level of protection. Not obvious or generic or merely descriptive, but something that is unique and source identifying. While registration is not required, it can bolster the value of the look and feel of the restaurant as intellectual property. Keep in mind that the same applies to a retail location. If you design a store that is so unique and distinctive and not obvious, then it may be protected as intellectual property and you can stop others from infringing on this unique design.

Second, the more challenging component—is it functional or does it goes beyond merely functional? Obviously, an arrangement of racks in a store or tables and chairs is likely to be merely functional. But a specific color display or unique art displays throughout the store, something that not only connects with your consumer at a fundamental level but is so different and unique that it could only be you, will become nonfunctional.

The consumer experience when shopping online becomes even more related to the brand identification and what the brand does to connect to the consumer. The online experience is as important to the brand as the in-store experience. Some of the most powerful retail brands have created a powerhouse online revenue stream, such as Barnes and Noble or Amazon One Click. The online storefront can also be protected by a blend of copyright law and trade dress law, following much of the same principles discussed in this chapter. The online characteristics must be unique and distinctive as source indicators for consumers. As online shopping becomes not only more prevalent but the norm, the need to protect consumers from false web sites or copiers will become more important. Careful attention to the online storefront and protecting it from counterfeiting is more important than ever.

An interesting of use of intellectual property to protect the setting is British Airways. British Airways developed a unique and patentable arrangement of seats in business class. It patented the configuration, but more importantly marketed and branded it as a unique differentiator in the experience of the consumer.

The Consumer Experience

The consumer experience can be protected through specialized operations manuals and training programs. While they can be copyrighted as tangible original written works, if the ideas presented are truly unique, you may want to use trade secret law to protect your training and operations guide. To do so, ensure that every participant in your training process signs a nondisclosure agreement. A good sample nondisclosure agreement is shown in Appendix C. The Ritz-Carlton, Disney, Nordstrom, Tiffany, all provide their consumers a unique experience from beginning to end. Capturing that in the form of intellectual property can further bolster the value of the company.

The Employee Experience

Remember, too, your internal communication can be branded and have an equally powerful impact. By branding key guiding principles within the company, your company will benefit from better informed employees, potentially becoming happier with their jobs, thus resulting in happier consumers ("If you take care of your employees, they will take care of your consumers"). Develop a marketing story so compelling that people will want to work for you and those who already do will carry themselves with pride. The employee experience sets the tone and creates a shared vision for how your team members deliver the experience to your consumers. At all levels of the company, branding the vision is important. At Kraft Foods, they use "Make Today Delicious."

A great example of an internal branding campaign is from The Limited. The Limited brands shifted to a "Shared-Services Model," evolving from interbrand competition within the company to a collaborative model. In order to effect this cultural shift, the company created "The Guide," a catalog of all employee tools across brands. In doing so, they used a fashion magazine metaphor (including "ads" from each retail division so that individual brands would be recognized and internal PR campaigns with posters and postcards). "The Guide" became the most successful internal communications campaign in company history.

The creative process requires extensive research, time, and most importantly, those gifted with creativity. Intersecting strategic thinking about what creates powerful intellectual property will enhance the outcome and the return on investment. This chapter has focused largely on an overview of how a campaign can be protected. More attention will be paid to how the process can work, tapping into the multidisciplinary teams at work in most companies.

> Everything should be made as simple as possible, but not simpler.
>
> ALBERT EINSTEIN

Chapter Highlights

- A powerful brand is one that provides a strong identification and connection between a consumer and the brand through its name, logo, visual identity, sights, sounds, touch, smell—all aspects of the consumer experience must consistently reinforce an emotional belief about the brand.
- Intellectual property protection of a brand campaign can include patents, trademarks/trade dress, trade secrets, and copyright protection.
- The creative process must adapt to intersect key strategic questions related to intellectual property during the creative

development in order to maximize results and intellectual property value.

- Product designs and package designs can be protected by design patents, trademark/trade dress, and sometimes copyright law. The design must be unique, distinctive, and nonfunctional.
- The name and logo of a brand remain at its foundation and are protected by trademark law. Global protection is necessary, requiring comprehensive searching of new names in their product categories. Trademarks should be beyond descriptive and provide a unique, arbitrary, or fanciful name with clear ability to obtain protection in the intended product categories around the globe.
- A fundamental premise behind trademark law is that it is intended to protect consumers so that they do not mistakenly buy one product thinking that it is another. Trademarks are reserved for those companies that invest in building a consumer connection with their name, logo, design, and so on. The trademark examiners do not want trademarks that might confuse consumers as to the product's origins.
- All aspects of a campaign can be protected. Unique and distinctive sounds can be trademarked. Music can be copyrighted. The commercial or print ad can be copyrighted. Characters can be both trademarked and copyrighted. Chefs and their signature dishes can also be trademarked.
- The retail environment, if not functional and unique, can be protected by trade dress law.
- Training programs and internal campaigns can be protected by copyright law, trademark law, or trade secret law. If any aspect of a training program is protected by trade secret law, it must be protected through the use of confidentiality or noncompete agreements.

4

The Influencers

Throughout our research, it became clear that a few trends and notable authors are influencing what our thought leaders are thinking and doing in their businesses. Some of the favorite reads of our interview subjects include: *Blue Ocean Strategy* by W. Chan Kim and Renee Mauborgne, Seth Godin's series of books, Malcom Gladwell's series of books, *The Game Changer* by A.G. Lafley, *Burning the Ships* by Marshall Phelps, *Built to Last* by Jim Collins and Jerry Porras, *Open Innovation* by Henry Chesbrough, as well as classics like the books of Peter Drucker.

We found that the following trends are driving the thinking of our innovative leaders and influencing their decision making:

Consumer-based insights

Content as marketing

Cost of litigation, risk, and uncertainty

The dilution dilemma

Limited budgets

Consumer-Based Insights

As consumers, we have everything we need and want. To break through and continue to grow, businesses must innovate at the consumer level with a deep understanding of consumers and how they live their life. Consumers may not yet know what they want or need or how it may change the way they live their lives. That's why companies exist, to continually innovate by understanding what was once unknown will become hot and in demand. This means we must be creating something that is new, innovative, and that captures consumer attention. And it means we must create processes and provide leadership with a single purpose and vision that facilitates understanding consumers.

In *Blue Ocean Strategy*, Kim and Mauborgne (2005) advocate abandoning old-school ways of simply looking to beat the competitors in the existing market space and instead look to create new space by thinking outside the box. They encourage companies to look at new sources of consumers, new market spaces, and innovate by understanding the needs and wants of people are not being met in order to create new and clear blue oceans.

Likewise, Seth Godin (2003) analogizes that if we continue to see the black and white cow as we drive along, we pay little attention, but a purple cow would surely get our attention. He argues that the only way to break through the clutter is to carve out new marketplaces.

The legendary Peter Drucker was a consummate advocate of the philosophy that the purpose of a company is to create a consumer and that all aspects of management and leadership must reinforce that guiding principle. He further believed in the importance of broadening the knowledge of company leaders. "Far too many people—especially people with great expertise in one area—are contemptuous of knowledge in other areas or believe that being bright is a substitute for knowledge. First-rate engineers, for instance, tend to take pride in not knowing anything about people. . . . Human resource professionals, by contrast, often pride themselves on their ignorance of elementary accounting. . . . But taking pride in such ignorance is self-defeating."

> Irene Rosenfeld, Kraft Foods' Chairman and CEO, really set the tone from the top down that innovation was important. When company leadership understands the importance of innovation from the consumer level, the entire company falls into step with that way of thinking. What you stand for and how you connect with consumers is more important than what you make or how you make it.
>
> JACQUELINE LEIMER,
> Distinguished IP Practitioner, Chicago-Kent College of Law,
> Former VP and Associate General Counsel, Kraft Foods,
> Former President, International Trademark Association

Businesses absolutely have to evolve. Not only do consumers demand more from them, but as patents expire or market needs change and your product line becomes obsolete, innovation must be constantly occurring by understanding the market. There is no question the trend in moving into a consumer-based innovation model has been occurring for many years.

Herbal Essences is a great success story from Procter & Gamble of taking a failing product, learning what consumers want and need, and turning it from worst to first. They understood that by repackaging, rebranding, and repositioning it to deliver consumers something they wanted in a way they could connect [to it, it would] translate into real economic value and return on investment. Focusing on the intrinsic value of the product to the consumer will deliver the greatest results.

Too many companies are focused on short-term gains versus longer term investment. This is what happened to the auto industry. They worked so hard to cut their costs to compete with foreign automakers that they lost touch with what their consumers want.

CRAIG VOGEL,
Assistant Dean, Design, Architecture,
Art and Planning, University of Cincinnati

David Ogilvy, the founder of legendary advertising agency Ogilvy & Mather, wrote that understanding the consumer was everything. If you didn't understand every aspect of how the product would work in the life of the consumer, you would miss it. In his famous Rolls-Royce print ad campaign, he invested countless hours working with the engineers who made the car, understanding every aspect of what the consumer would experience. It led to the famous headline: "At 60 miles an hour, the loudest noise in this new Rolls-Royce comes from the ticking of its electric clock."

Every time you get into trouble it's because you lose touch with your consumer. Every time you hit a home run, it's because you are listening carefully to your consumer. Tapping into the power of consumers was something we always did at P&G.

All of the best ideas come from the consumer. One of our successes was the turn-around of Secret. The campaign: *Strong enough for a man, but made for a woman* came out of women's expressions of their need. We also protected Downey while launching Bounce Fabric Softener, no easy feat, and impossible without consumer understanding. We understood keenly, though, the difference in the consumers and why they would choose one product over the other. Bounce consumers wanted to eliminate static cling. Downey consumers wanted soft clothes that smelled nice.

Bob Wehling,
Former Global Marketing Officer, Procter & Gamble

If you have full team participation up front, your claims in the ad campaign can be that much stronger. Think about how much better it is if the ad people can talk to the engineers who invented the product. They often understand better than anyone what the product can and cannot do and not only avoid making costly mistakes, the full team will have more knowledge and power to make better informed decisions with better output.

Jeff Weedman,
Vice President, Global Business
Development, Procter & Gamble

In the food industry, technology has not been *the only* driver of top line growth. Understanding our consumer and solving a critical need does *drive growth*. Many solutions to consumer needs have not been technology oriented.

Heidi Emanuel,
Senior Innovation Officer, General Mills

While it may seem obvious that we must innovate and develop new ideas from the consumer experience level, it is the obvious that sometimes can get lost in company politics, bureaucracy, budget cuts, and the like. It is also the obvious that can become genius and brilliant when it is implemented and integrated into a daily way of life in a company, producing outstanding returns. Constantly reinforcing this simple guiding principle in everything we do is essential to improving the return on investment of innovation and branding activities. The leadership of a company must set this as a priority and consider the cultural changes needed to indoctrinate this philosophy at all levels of the company.

> Good ideas can come from anywhere in the company. We try to facilitate that belief and encourage ideas to percolate up at all levels.

> A.B. Cruz III,
> Executive Vice President, Chief Legal Officer, and
> Corporate Secretary, Scripps Networks Interactive, Inc.

Content as Marketing

In the age of Facebook, YouTube, Twitter, and Barack Obama's rise to success through an unprecedented e-mail and grassroots electronic political campaign, modern marketing is all about creating content, programs, and aggregating information that is customized to each and every consumer. We all expect everything to be tailored to what we want and need when we want and need it and no longer respond to mass advertising messages. Effective campaigns undoubtedly involve some aspect of content creation targeted to its consumer. This is not, however, a new idea.

Consider for a moment the original soap opera. The name itself is derived from its source—a daytime drama sponsored by and created by soap companies in order to sell their products to housewives of the 1950s and 1960s. Soap operas actually originated on the radio in 15-minute segments airing each day with a dangling thread to keep women tuning back in. With television, the concept evolved into a new form of storytelling wrapped by an ad campaign. At that time most women stayed at home with children, and television was so new that daytime programming was needed.

In a brilliant move by the ad agencies of the time, whole programs were created and sponsored by soap companies that were tailored to their consumers' interests and needs. By creating stories filled with romance, intrigue, cat fights, and showcasing women at their best and worst, the soap companies tapped in to the power of connecting with their consumers and creating a fantasy for them. As the drama cuts to commercial right at a pivotal moment, the fantasy begins. A beautiful woman in a flowing dress wearing pearls is doing laundry for her family in her cute little house with the white picket fence—what every woman wanted at the time, or at least the advertisers wanted them to think so.

Today, it's a bit more complex than that. Although moms may still be a primary market for soap products, niched consumer groups have emerged as our society embraces diversity in lifestyles. Buying power has shifted and new markets, driven often by the younger generation, demand more. Likewise, the baby boomers continue to be a huge market segment targeted by many companies.

> All too often, I think marketers discount the importance of the 50+ age group. These are the influencers and maintain the largest amount of purchasing power. To ignore them is a mistake. You don't suddenly go brain dead and decide not to try new or improved products when you turn 50 or even 70.
>
> BOB WEHLING,
> Former Global Marketing Officer, Procter & Gamble

Marketers now must be a bit savvier and need people in their target audience to help connect with their consumers. Frito-Lay launched what is now considered one of the most successful public relations campaigns of contemporary times. In 2007, Doritos sponsored its first, and now annual, Crash the Super Bowl Campaign. This multifaceted campaign included a contest in which consumers could create their own Super Bowl ad. Yahoo!, YouTube, and MySpace delivered a casting call to Doritos enthusiasts. Consumers could then view and vote for their favorites on www.crashthesuperbowl.com. For the first time on the most-watched program, the Super Bowl, the consumer was in charge. Doritos has continued to be at the forefront of engaging consumers in the creation of messaging. Doritos launched the music career of one of its talented fans by airing her original song in a music video during Super Bowl XLII air time as part of its second annual Crash the Super Bowl. In 2009, the consumer-generated ad earned the coveted number one spot on *USA Today*'s Annual Super Bowl Ad Meter. This type of campaign not only engages consumers in the brand and creates content they want to see over and over, but generates enough free air time in public relations to pay for the cost of the Super Bowl ad itself. Not bad for a Super Bowl campaign that breaks the budget for most companies.

Extensive product placement in movies, too, has become a way to tie programming into a subliminal advertising message. Knowing that ET eats Reese's Pieces in 1982 was just the beginning. Even small independent films are often saturated with products hoping to connect to their prospective consumers.

Disney is another prime example of using content to promote its products and services. Disney, as a mega-entertainment company, cross promotes every facet of its business through the use of its celebrities, stories, characters, and never-ending belief that Disney is magic. Also, owning ABC, the company conveniently places its celebrities on its reality shows such as *Dancing with the Stars* and uses ad time to promote its other products. It turns its actors into musicians and promotes their music during commercial breaks. Those same voices then show up in animated feature films. Disney brilliantly cross sells its theme parks, vacation experiences, toys and merchandise, movies, music, and other programming across every channel. It has created content to drive the sale of its other products. In fact, the entire Disney Channel is really one big ad for Disney products. Although its founding as an entertainment company may have made that an easier model to put in place, other companies can take an important page out of the Disney book. If you can tap into what your consumers want to watch, read, and hear and give them content that meets those needs, your message about your product is not only more likely to break through the clutter, but it is likely to become a part of their lifestyle.

Likewise, the Food Network and HGTV have successfully turned chefs and interior designers into celebrities and leveraged television shows to also promote books and products related to cooking and home improvement, creating new revenue sources for the company, all rooted in the content it provides.

> We definitely see our advertisers looking for more product placement, product-based programming, and new ways to connect their product with their consumers. They are looking for interactive ways to build a community with their consumers. As a highly branded network company, we look for how we can partner with our advertisers to make that happen.
>
> A.B. Cruz III,
> Executive Vice President, Chief Legal Officer, and
> Corporate Secretary, Scripps Networks Interactive, Inc.

One of the biggest challenges marketers face today is having one foot in traditional media and the other in digital media. They each remain important.

Bob Wehling,
Former Global Marketing Officer, Procter & Gamble

Not only are consumers responding more to content-based promotions, but with their ability to fast forward through commercials, build their own entertainment playlists, and circumvent the traditional advertising media. The need to create content that the consumer wants is pivotal to conveying the message and building the brand. This trend will continue and expand. Savvy branding professionals will recognize that they must be creating the soap opera for their market. Designing a promotional message into highly demanded content will be one key to success in the next generation of branding. And with that content creation comes a greater need for protection of that content on a global level. Not only must the content be protected to avoid dilution, but every aspect of what is created must be carefully structured so that it is owned by the company. Work-for-hire agreements, licensing agreements, and the like are just one piece of that puzzle.

Cost of Litigation, Risk, and Uncertainty

With the continued and rapid development of new technologies, the legislators and courts cannot keep up with changing laws needed to address the new legal issues that arise from the use of technology. There is very little predictability in litigation other than one simple truth—it will cost you hundreds of thousands to millions of dollars to litigate an intellectual property matter. With a strong proactive intellectual property strategy, your company can avoid or at least be prepared for any litigation by knowing how and why you are protecting your products, services, and marketing campaigns and knowing how or why you are infringing on the rights of others. Following are a few key emerging areas of potential lawsuits that directly affect the creation of a brand campaign:

> *Meta Data and Key Words.* A heavily contentious new question is whether a company can use a competitor's name in the meta-data of its web site or in a key word search for its web

site. Although there are layers of legal arguments on both sides of this question, the reality is that for branding professionals, the potential exists for what they are doing to ultimately result in lawsuits against the company. The bottom line is that there should be regular discussion with intellectual property lawyers to stay on top of current law and be prepared to modify strategies to avoid or minimize exposure to lawsuits. There is no question, however, that using a competitor's trademark or brand name in any way, shape, or form can expose you to potential liability. Understanding the safe harbors and making informed risk–based decisions as a team can minimize unexpected costs.

Patent Trolls. "Patent trolls" have emerged from the depths to seek the deep pockets of American corporations for a quick payout. Techies seek patent protection of various systems and methods related to basic interactive web sites and then file lawsuits against any and every company potentially infringing upon their patent in order to obtain a quick windfall. Companies, however, recognize that settling with even one troll will only lead to more suits of the same kind. It becomes even more important for companies to consider proactive campaigns to avoid these patent trolls. For example, many of the companies we talked to aggressively pursue their own patents for the specific purpose of battling these trolls on their turf.

Sharing of Digital Files. The music industry fought the good fight and lost. While Apple found the consumer-based solution (making it cheap and easy to buy, download, and organize digital files), the music titans rearranged deck chairs on the *Titanic.* Some issues have been resolved, but the continued proliferation of digital content will require continued evolution of global copyright laws to control the dissemination of content.

Cyber Squatting. In the early days of commercial use of the internet, cyber squatters (those who acquire famous names as web sites in order to charge the rightful owner to obtain the domain name) made headlines. Today the problem remains but in an ever-changing way. According to DictionaryOne, at this juncture almost every known word in the English language has been tapped into as a domain name. Cyber squatting continues to be an issue. It is important to ensure that you carefully evaluate availability on all domain extensions and obtain trademark protection in order to stop a cyber squatter.

Work-for-Hire/License Agreements. Whenever using creative work created by another person or company, it is mission critical to have in place a valid contract that makes the product a work for hire. That means, if you pay for it, you own it and all rights associated with it. Additionally, as more companies jointly develop products and services or cross promote and sell their complementary products, a carefully constructed license agreement that contemplates all aspects of liability and infringement is all the more important. Further, as licensing intellectual property becomes a new source of revenue for companies, it can also become a source of litigation. Executives, branding professionals, and lawyers must work in a multidisciplinary fashion to ensure that future company goals are not compromised in license agreements.

Rights of Privacy/Publicity/User-Generated Content. Any use of a person, whether a private person or a famous person, will require the appropriate releases in order to be used. For any user-generated content, the appropriate releases must be obtained through the terms and conditions of the site and appropriate measures to remedy concerns. Likewise, the use of any name or likeness of a famous person requires the permission of that famous person. While it may be easier today to create a voice-over sounding like someone famous or use Photoshop to insert the person you want in a picture, doing so violates the person's rights and can subject you to lawsuits. Although this may be less of a problem at the professional level, when tapping into user-generated content where those safeguards are not in place, careful vetting must become part of any contest, promotion, or process. A brief caveat: The only exception is that free speech provides the right to parody. If you are simply making a parody of a celebrity and not intending to mislead consumers that the celebrity has endorsed your product, then it is free speech rather than a violation. It's a fine line with many nuances, so good counsel is important on this issue.

International Protection. Any campaign that will be used to promote a global brand must consider appropriate protection and registration requirements and infringement potential in countries around the globe.

Consumer Free Speech vs. Infringement. This is becoming an ever-increasing area of concern. While cult-like brands such as Doritos, Harry Potter, Chipotle, and others may want their loyal consumers to build communities around their products, they must carefully weigh whether free speech about their product crosses over into harmful infringement. Most famously, *Saturday Night Live* sought to remove its clips from YouTube, only to realize that perhaps it was not a bad thing that people were seeking their content. Brand owners now, more than ever, must carefully evaluate whether misuse of their brand names by their followers does more harm than good and determine the cost benefit of pursuing infringers.

Children's Online Rights. The Children's Online Protection Act was enacted in 2000 to protect children under the age of 13. The rules spell out what a web site operator must include in a privacy policy, when and how to seek verifiable consent from a parent, and what responsibilities an operator has to protect children's privacy and safety online. The Federal Trade Commission enforces these rules and may seek extensive civil penalties for violation of them.

Violation of Other Rights in Traditional IP. In addition to the previous new areas of law, the traditional question of whether any activity by the company will violate traditional patent, copyright, trademark, and trade secret law is still an essential part of launching any campaign.

For most companies, settling lawsuits early will only give rise to other lawsuits by similar predators. With the continued rising costs associated with litigating, companies must carefully assess exposure to risk. The need for careful risk assessment when launching any campaign that could potentially cause litigation must be considered as part of the return on investment. Additionally, once a lawsuit is filed against a company, it becomes public record, which will ultimately impact the stock market if the lawsuit has the potential to be costly, out of the ordinary, and disruptive.

> Freedom to operate is a critical issue, not just in patent-related matters, but across the board. We need to fully vet any idea to ensure it does not expose us to costly lawsuits. Failing to fully evaluate the ability to utilize an idea in the global market-place not only wastes the money it takes to develop the idea, but wastes precious time that could be spent investing in new ideas and products. Further, the cost of litigation is spiraling out of control. Our primary goal in working with our business partners is to ensure that we have the freedom to operate, first and foremost, and then work collaboratively to ensure we can maximize the protection of the ideas.
>
> GREGG MARRAZZO,
> Vice President and Chief Counsel,
> Intellectual Property and Global Marketing, Kimberly-Clark

> Unfortunately, many companies don't recognize the cost of litigation until a crisis hits, then suddenly everyone understands the role of risk management. As a branding lawyer, I work very hard to apprise our chief marketing officer and business team of risks and provide case studies or remind them of when and how things can go really wrong. The good ones will get it and know that even if they have moved on to another position when the crisis hits, they don't want to be the one who disregarded the risk analysis and moved forward without clear strategic reasons to do so.
>
> RUBY ZEFO,
> Director, Trademarks and Brands, Intel

The Dilution Dilemma

Forward-thinking companies understand the importance and urgency of protecting innovation to compete in the marketplace and to sustain that competitive advantage long enough to recognize the desired return on investment. Failure to capture the sustainability can destroy the anticipated ROI from innovation.

In the development stage of innovation and branding, careful consideration must be given to the plan to minimize potential dilution and counterfeiting in the marketplace. This requires a forward-looking approach to how a brand is protected, exploited, and protected. There are many examples of dilution.

For example, consider a wide range of famous consumer products that have largely been replaced in the average grocery store with private labels by the grocer. Examples range from your favorite food products, fresh meat and poultry, to cosmetics and paper products. If consumers are not regularly reminded through advertising and branding campaigns of the difference between the private label and the premium brand, the consumer will simply choose the store's private label brand rather than the premium brand. This can ultimately cause a decrease in brand value, resulting in an impairment of that intellectual asset on the balance sheet of its owner, not to mention reduced sales and weaker shelf placement in the grocery store.

Additionally, from the intellectual property perspective, the premium brand has run the risk of not just marketplace dilution, but trademark dilution, where the name is no longer a source indicator to its owner and thus subject to dilution. The company may lose its valuable trademark rights to the name. If the term becomes common and used for all types of this product, it not only loses market share and brand recognition with consumers, but legally and in valuation terms it loses most if not all of its value and results in impairment on the balance sheet. This is just one example of potential dilution if the investment is not continually made in the brand.

Also important to consider in the dilution dilemma is the impact of counterfeiting. This has long plagued the entertainment and fashion industry with bootlegged versions of movies, music, games, counterfeit handbags, shoes, and the like being sold on the street, and it has extended into other areas of business. According to the International Anti-Counterfeiting Coalition, counterfeiting costs U.S. businesses $200 billion to $250 billion annually. Counterfeit merchandise is directly responsible for the loss of more than 750,000 American jobs and approximately 5–7 percent of world trade is in counterfeit goods. Of more concern, the Federal Aviation Administration estimates that 2 percent of the 26 million airline parts installed each year are counterfeit, and the Food and

Drug Administration estimates that 10 percent of all drugs sold in the United States are counterfeit. Brand owners are largely required to police the world themselves and prosecute infringers and counterfeiters. This has created an industry centered on spotting and prosecuting counterfeiters.

> I believe technology and globalization are going to continue to make things both better and worse. Obviously, technology has helped counterfeiters replicate products more quickly and cost-effectively, and globalization has enabled this process from production to consumers in ever-expanding markets. Conversely, I see technology solutions related to packaging, tagging, tracking, and investigating product counterfeiting and counterfeiters as improving radically in coming years. As costs of counterfeit production go up, profits go down, and as intellectual property rights becomes more of a priority for law enforcement, risk of capture and incarceration is more of a reality.
>
> VINCE VOLPI,
> Chair and CEO, Pica, a global anti-counterfeiting company

The damage caused by allowing a counterfeiter to sell your brand: irreparable. All of the intellectual property protections discussed in this book and available to companies require a level of diligence to maintain the value of those assets. While there are increasing efforts by various organizations globally to assist and facilitate enforcement activity, there is not exactly an intellectual property police force that you can call on to tackle this problem. Companies and leaders in the industry must address these issues and budget for them in the overall planning process. The brand must be protected globally in order for it to be sustained.

> While many of our clients get frustrated by corruption or what they see as state-sponsored or condoned counterfeiting, this does not mean that you disengage. You have to build successful intellectual property rights strategies, in some cases, one brick at a time. As intellectual property becomes more of a global priority for countries desiring free trade, access to markets, and external investment, there will be more pressure to police

product counterfeiting, and you can only take advantage of this if you are engaged. Additionally, as the world shrinks and information becomes more widely available to all, more advocates and activists will get the message out to more consumers about the perils of counterfeit products and the "collateral damage" (supporting organized crime, human trafficking, tax fraud, loss of jobs and investment) from even ostensibly "victimless" counterfeit activity such as the production of fake luxury goods.

VINCE VOLPI,
Chair and CEO, PICA, a global anti-counterfeiting company

An important aspect of every brand is the cost of what it takes to protect it globally. You can't really build a brand without thinking strategically about enforcement globally. Vigorous enforcement is required. To effectively carry this out, it must be part of the discussion at the front end of the brand plan.

NILS MONTAN,
Former Chief Trademark Counsel, Warner Bros.,
Former President, International Trademark Association,
Former President, International AntiCounterfeiting Association

New products may become a piece of art or an iconic symbol such as Herman Miller furniture, Apple computers, Apple iPod, and Apple iPhone, or Hermes bags. Companies must strategically evaluate not only how to innovate in a brilliant way that creates new consumers or market space, but also how to utilize the protections available in the process to ensure that they can stop the copying of designs or ideas globally. The protection plan cannot be an afterthought; it must be built into the process. Companies engaged in anticounterfeiting can find support from the International Anti Counterfeiting Coalition and the International Trademark Association.

By focusing on our core brands and simplifying our message, it becomes more cost effective for global protection and maintenance of our brand.

RUBY ZEFO,
Director, Trademarks and Brands, Intel

Limited Budgets

As budgets shrink in the aftermath of an economic crisis, executives are pushing their branding professionals and legal departments to think differently. When we work in multidisciplinary teams with the right person facilitating the discussions, we get better, more efficient results that are more likely to achieve the goal with less money and less likely to result in unexpected litigation or costs. It's really that simple.

The term *new economy* was used in the early 2000s to mean pouring a ton of cash into an Internet start-up with outrageous valuations, spending widely on rapid growth. Now, it means streamlined overhead, reduced costs, more use of outside experts and outside resources, open and collaborative innovation, and consumer-driven products and services.

How budgets are allocated will have an impact on how a team can or cannot work together. At some companies, the budgeting is decentralized to allow for more accountability and evaluation of return on investment for how the budget was used.

It's all about calculating and measuring the return on investment. The cost of development, whether in technology or marketing, must produce a return. It must avoid lawsuits, it must cost less, and it must produce greater monetization. *The way in which companies allocate budgets and provide incentives or penalize groups and departments will clearly have an impact on all of these issues. We found consistently in our research that a fundamental truth of every organization is that every one of us is motivated by how we get ahead in our respective careers.* Companies can foster and facilitate incentive programs that feed into collaboration and higher return on investment or they can remain trapped in antiquated ways of providing incentives to people.

The Brand Rewired approach means that the money invested in a new product, service, design, or brand has a greater chance of connecting with consumers, has a greater chance of global protection with less exposure to counterfeiting and/or dilution, has less of a chance of being involved in litigation, and the money spent in creating and building the brand has a greater chance of producing the expected return.

As companies evaluate more cost-effective means to distribute their products and services through licensing and distribution strategies with other parties globally, the need for a carefully crafted intellectual property strategy evaluating how a brand is protected in a cost-effective means globally is required in order to minimize costs and increase return.

The Brand Rewired approach will not only reduce costs in internal processes and reduce costs in the use of outside professionals by eliminating the silo mentality through multidisciplinary teams, but also will create something of greater long-term economic value.

Bottom line: This process helps you do more with less.

> Beware of little expenses. A small leak will sink a great ship.
>
> BENJAMIN FRANKLIN

Chapter Highlights

- Consumers have everything they need. To compete in the global marketplace, companies must innovate by understanding the consumer lifestyle and find opportunities to provide products and services to consumers, even if they do not yet know they want those products or services.
- Thought leaders in the industry advocate that companies are about creating consumers and that to survive, they must think differently than just about beating competitors in an existing market space and must tap into new market opportunities.
- In the mid-20th century, advertisers made their mark on society by creating campaigns that would saturate the media of the time with messages that created a fantasy for their consumers. This traditional advertising message gave consumers of the time an emotional connection to products or services through the ad campaign fantasy.
- Today, consumers are in the driver's seat. They can fast forward through just about any message and create their own entertainment playlists of TV shows, movies, music, games, and more.

- Savvy marketers now recognize they must create content that the consumer will seek and embed their promotional messages within that content.
- The proliferation of promotional-based content requires greater understanding of the many intellectual property issues associated with protection and capitalizing on the content, as well as the products and services themselves. Multidisciplinary teams are needed to bridge the many issues that must be considered in this new way of marketing.
- The cost of litigation, risk, and uncertainty continues to rise. As new technologies rapidly evolve, new forms of lawsuits emerge. With the cost of the average lawsuit in the hundreds of thousands to millions of dollars, risk assessment must be integrated in the brand campaign development process in a proactive manner.
- The dilution dilemma continues to plague popular brands throughout the world as counterfeits and knock-offs can dilute the value of the brand.
- If brands fail to invest in continued marketing and maintenance, they may find that retailers no longer shelve their products prominently, so that they lose further market share and their value is diminished.
- Branding companies must carefully police and protect their brands throughout the world to ensure they do not lose their ability to enforce their rights while also continuing to market and promote their brands as a continual investment in consumer loyalty.
- Limited budgets have damaged the ability of companies to invest in their brands the way they once did. They must make smarter decisions about the use of resources. This requires new ways of thinking. Multidisciplinary teams can bring creative thinking and ideas on how to continue to tap into new market opportunities, while reinforcing and building the power of their brands.

CHAPTER 5

The Black Box

The term *black box* can have many meanings. In aviation, the "black box" is the box responsible for recording flight parameters and holds the cockpit voice recorder. The phrase became popularized by modern media reporting on aircraft crashes. In computing, a black box program is one whose inner workings are invisible to the user or one that has no side effects and whose function need not be examined, a routine suitable for reuse. In philosophy and psychology, the school of behaviorism sees the human mind as a black box. In corporations, however, the black box phenomenon refers to the silos that tend to exist and to how decisions may be made in a black box without input from other disciplines within the company.

This chapter examines the dangers that can occur if innovation, branding, and development occur within the silos or black box. A Brand Rewired approach to innovation and brand development creates processes and systems to avoid the results of a black box theory.

Consider the silo approach to brand and product development we discussed at the beginning of the book (see Figure 5.1).

Figure 5.1 represents a black box mentality. In this model, each subject matter expert offers expertise in his or her given area, but lacking important information from other disciplines, thus operating in a silo. Let's examine what happens when companies operate within silos and the black box phenomenon casts a shadow over the company.

Executive Leadership

Sets business strategy for growth of company.

Decides when to move beyond R&D and into commercial deployment.

Determines cost-benefit and risk analysis for moving forward with campaign.

Research & Development

Develops new products and services.

Reports to Executive Leadership providing recommendations.

Patent Counsel

Provides opinion on patentability/ freedom to practice—applies for patents.

Marketing

Brand/Ad Agency

Creates branding and marketing campaigns for commercial deployment based upon consumer research.

Reports to Executive Leadership providing recommendations.

Trademark/Advertising Counsel

Provides opinion on whether campaign will infringe on rights of others and availability of trademarks—applies for trademarks.

Figure 5.1   The Silo Approach

To illustrate this point, rather than ask any one company to share its black box stories, we thought it more efficient to pull from all of our research and create a fictional case study to demonstrate what could go wrong if operating in a black box. This short story will lay the groundwork for our case study in both a black box and a Brand Rewired approach. Typically the time frame to develop and launch a new product is two to three years. For these purposes, we will accelerate this process.

A Fictional Case Study—Emerson Jones

The Emerson Jones Company has been in business for more than two generations. Originally founded as a plastics company, Emerson Jones made plastic displays used in a variety of retail and commercial settings. The company was a privately owned family business and had long held traditional conservative values. It had become quietly successful over the years.

The second-generation owner, Emerson Jones Jr., observed an interesting trend in the 1980s, creating a new opportunity for his business. As an obsession with fitness and health took hold in

American society, he recognized that people were drinking more water and carrying around bottled water.

Working with his research and development team he quickly figured that he could retool his facility to start producing cheap, throwaway plastic bottles to meet the increasing demand for bottled water. He could recover the costs of financing the retooling in the first year of operation of the new facility with high margins thereafter. He was one of the first companies in the market producing cheap plastic bottles and become an instant millionaire, producing plastic bottles for the major beverage companies. He was very proud of the innovative thinking his company had demonstrated in spotting this opportunity and turning it into financial success.

Years later, while his business enjoyed steady annual growth and expanded significantly, an important event occurred, dramatically impacting his outlook on the business that had brought him his fortune.

He and his wife were birders and photographers traveling the world on adventure trips to pursue their passion. Also an observant consumer, he studied business trends with great interest and prided himself on finding innovative ideas during his adventures. Emerson and his wife were hiking when they came across a bird struggling to breathe because of a plastic ring wrapped around its neck. Upon closer examination, he found that this ring likely originated in his facility along with the plastic bottles they produced. The reality that producing cheap, throwaway plastic bottles was destroying the environment began to take on a whole new meaning for Emerson. It was disturbing and weighed heavily on him as he traveled throughout the world and considered the legacy he would leave to his children and grandchildren. Although they were very wealthy and his family would want for nothing, he had contributed to the erosion of the environment in a dramatic and powerful way.

He set out on a journey to discover a solution to this problem. He believed that patience and thoughtful consideration was needed and that the answer would present itself to him. During one of his trips to South America, he observed villagers making tools from plastic bottles. His new idea was taking root. He was intrigued by the rudimentary recycling that was taking place in this village. The villagers explained that they reused everything and wasted nothing. These plastics could be used in many facets of their lives, and they took pride in the productive use of everything they touched.

These villagers were not bombarded with recycling campaigns and guilt-laden messages about the environment. There was simply a cultural acceptance that nothing was to be wasted. Everything was to be used to its fullest potential. Emerson had been an advocate and done his part in supporting traditional recycling, but he began to wonder if there might be another opportunity to tap into this feeling in America.

While recycling was a hot topic of discussion, many people failed to recycle because it was inconvenient or they couldn't touch and feel what the end result would be. Unlike the villagers, most Americans don't have a cultural belief that nothing should be wasted. They don't have an emotional connection or sense of pride in the reuse of bottles. What happened to those bottles once they were placed in the recycling bin? The average person had no idea and was disconnected from the outcome.

While returning home, Emerson realized what he needed to do. A consumer product line made of recycled plastics needed to be created. It needed to be something used in average daily life to have a greater impact. Not only would consumers be able to touch and feel the outcome, but they would be motivated by the fact that their recycled bottles could be reused for something valuable in their life. His mission was to create an emotional connection to the product and a cultural shift that everything can be reused in a meaningful way.

Emerson had some of the best engineers in the world working for him. He would challenge them to find products that could be made from recyclables and become a part of everyday life. Once they knew the products that could be created, his marketing team would develop a campaign to promote this new product line, and his finance team would figure out how to make it profitable.

He would build a brand and an exciting new product line that consumers would demand as part of their role in sustainability and cleaning up the planet.

He would help to undo what he had done. He was bubbling over with ideas and couldn't wait to get back to his team to begin work on his legacy project. He would find a way to reuse the plastic bottles in a unique way that would create excitement for the products and the environment.

He called his senior leadership team for a meeting and excitedly explained his vision. Naturally, everyone thought he was merely excited because of his recent travels, but they humored him as he described how he was going to save the world with this unique new product line.

He had the vision, but the team had to build the plan. What was this transformational product line? Where would they get the technology to shift from bottle production to recycling and repurposing? How would they finance it? How would they sell it to consumers? These were all questions to be answered.

The leadership team included members from research and development, marketing, finance, legal, and public relations. Research and development would take the lead in developing the product line and determining the engineering requirements for the plan.

Just as he had done before, he would repurpose his company to meet a new opportunity. And he just might make a difference for future generations.

Now that we've set the stage with our story, let's see what happens when each group functions in a black box.

Research and Development

The research and development (R&D) team went to work. With brilliant engineers who prided themselves on their ability to solve any scientific problem, they set out to determine what consumer product they could produce from recycled plastic bottles with limited costs in repurposing their facilities.

Plastic can be recycled into fibers and turned into many different types of products. The R&D department spent months and months testing various ideas and concluded that the most cost-effective solution was to create insulation for homes. They were confident this would meet the social goals of their CEO by creating something that would protect consumers from the outside elements—turning their bottles of water into the very stuff that keeps their homes warm in the winter.

In their research of the insulation market, they determined that if they could obtain just 5 percent of the market share of all insulation sold, they could finance this project and produce the necessary margin to replace the profits generated by bottle making. Excitedly they shared the idea with Emerson, who embraced the idea immediately. He would get to work with the finance team to determine how to finance the project and move this forward. In the meantime, in order to protect this important work and provide the greatest possible return, he instructed the R&D team to begin to patent every aspect of the technology and told the marketing team to get cracking on a new brand for their line of insulation so that they would be prepared to go to market as soon as the facility could be retooled. The patent lawyers got to work and analyzed whether they might infringe on any other patents, as well as how likely it might be to obtain patent protection globally. Since they had some concerns about potential infringement of another recycling company, they decided to work with the company owning the related patent and obtain a license agreement or joint development agreement with them. They wanted to avoid lawsuits if at all possible, so they took this very proactive approach.

While the R&D department has brilliantly created a new technology to accomplish the goal of the CEO and has the best possible intentions in moving this forward, just a few of the things that could go wrong when R&D is operating in a silo are the following:

- The cost to globally apply for, protect, and maintain the patents far outweighs any potential for return.
- The aspects of the technology that could be protected by trade secrets are shared with other companies without the appropriate disclosure agreements in place, thereby destroying any intellectual property value they had.
- The patents are applied for before the license agreement or joint development agreement is negotiated, and the company is later sued for patent infringement, which costs the company an unanticipated two million dollars for legal and settlement costs.
- Other insulation companies also manufacture products from recycled plastics, and there is no unique differentiator for consumers, resulting in the inability to earn the anticipated market share.

Marketing and Advertising Campaign

As the product emerged from R&D and was given a green light, the marketing and advertising experts were ready to shine with their creative and strategic thinking. While they were not crazy about the insulation product, they were committed to their company and their CEO, and they diligently got to work to develop a new name and a campaign to sell insulation with a social mission about improving the environment.

They hired the best in the business to coin the name and invested hundreds of thousands of dollars. Working closing with the brand agency, they explored hundred of names, arriving at one clear winner: Green Again Insulation. The name created an immediate connection to the environment through the use of *Green* and the term *Again* meant recycled. In fact, they checked with R&D and determined that they could even make the insulation green.

Emerson loved this idea. His vision of building a consumer product line of recycled plastic was beginning to take shape. Excited, he instructed the public relations department to begin to announce the new product line and social mission of this project.

In the meantime, he directed marketing to call the trademark lawyers to get this trademarked. The marketing team told the trademark attorney the name of the product, but neglected to tell them anything more. The trademark attorney promptly ran a search, finding another company using the name Green Again, but for a line of gardening products, which caused some concern; but given the large investment already spent in branding, they could proceed. The trademark was then pursued for Green Again in the insulation category.

The marketing team moved on to build a campaign to launch the product, feeling assured that the name for their new product

line would be protected. To compete with the Pink Panther character used for Owens Corning insulation, the team created a Green Tree character. Spending money with the best ad agencies in the world, they created a brilliant campaign featuring the talking Green Tree, a catchy jingle, and an interactive web site to help teach people of all ages how they could improve the environment. They even decided to create a Green Tree stuffed toy that would be given away with the insulation to connect kids (and their parents) to the idea that the Green Again insulation was keeping them safe and warm while they slept at night. Although they would be spending millions of dollars to launch this new product, they recognized that a celebrity voice as the Green Tree would simply cost too much and put them over budget. They decided to find someone with a voice similar to that of a famous actress to be the voice of the Green Tree.

The marketing team did a stellar job in coordinating naming agencies and ad agencies and in building a campaign to market their new line of Green Again Insulation. However, a few things that could go wrong or that might have been missed by operating in a black box are the following:

- Once the product was launched, other insulation companies quickly capitalized on the significant dollar investment Emerson Jones made in educating people about insulation made from recycled plastics, and competitors began to make their insulation green as well. Although this was Emerson Jones's idea, because they didn't trademark it (the trademark attorney didn't know it was going to be green), they can't easily stop others from doing it. The green color for insulation became commonplace in the market. They could have owned it and obtained the market share they needed, but failure to protect this simple, yet profound aspect of their product meant others could capitalize on their investment.
- The catchy jingle that was created was not protected or copyrighted early in the process. Other companies looking to tap into the consumer's emotional connection to doing what's right for the environment took key elements of that jingle and incorporated it into their own, further diluting the power of this campaign as unique and distinctive to Emerson Jones.
- The cute Green Tree character was also quickly replicated by other companies looking to demonstrate that they were

environmentally friendly. Although it was never copied exactly, other companies tapping into the Green Tree idea further diminished its distinctiveness to Emerson Jones. Although it could have been trademarked, it wasn't.

- The celebrity sound-alike voice sounded so much like the celebrity that the celebrity sued the company for infringing on her rights of publicity. With the law on her side, the company settled for millions of dollars and had to reproduce every single ad with a different voice. To overcome the public relations problem that followed, the company hired a new celebrity, legitimately, to be the voice and spent significantly more than anticipated to relaunch the campaign with the new celebrity voice as the Green Tree.

- To make matters worse, the ad campaign incorrectly cited statistics about other insulation companies, resulting in an FTC investigation and a fine. And the web site that offered free games to kids featuring the Green Tree failed to follow the ever-changing guidelines of the Children's Online Protection Act. The company spent even more money to correct the ads and rebuild consumer trust in the Green Again brand.

- Other companies wanting to build on the vast investment in consumer awareness made by Emerson Jones began to name their product packages Green Again. With a limited scope of trademark protection in the insulation product category, Emerson Jones was unable to stop the complete dilution of its brand into a household name for "made from recycled plastics." Although the goal was for it to be a household name, it was now a household name that everyone was using and it had no unique connection to Emerson Jones anymore.

While the campaign was brilliant, failure to involve the right people in the discussion earlier resulted in additional costs and lost value to the company.

Public Relations and Investor Relations

Emerson Jones was excited about the marketing campaign that his team had developed. Confident this would achieve his business and social mission, he was ready for the public relations team to begin announcing the new product line to the world. While they had always been a private company, he and his finance team decided that if this new product line went well, they might be able to go public and he could leave his legacy to the world.

The PR team was instructed to begin sending out news releases about the new technology, new product line, and pending campaign. Getting the business publications talking about Emerson Jones would be critical to the company's opportunity to go public.

They interviewed the R&D department to understand more about the technology and the marketing team about the pending campaign to launch the product. They quickly went to work preparing news releases, updating the company web site, and pitching the story to the major business publications. They were hugely successful. The *Wall Street Journal, BusinessWeek,* even *Fast Company* wanted to do a story on this social mission that was guiding the changes in the company.

The PR department had done an excellent job of driving interest in the story. But without involvement as a team with other departments, a few problems could develop.

- By announcing the green color of the insulation in the news release, they alerted competitors to the idea before it hit the market. Quickly confirming that no trademark had been filed, other companies moved to implement the green color in their own manufacturing to indicate that they were also environmentally friendly.
- In a quote provided by one of the R&D professionals, the aspect of the process that was unique and could have been protected by trade secret law was publicly announced, thereby eliminating any ability to ever protect it as a trade secret.
- The unions that managed the workers in the plant were unaware that plans were in development to repurpose the plant for a new function. Although Emerson Jones had no intention of changing its workforce, the union was outraged that they had not been consulted about this change in thinking. The company now faced significant problems with its labor force.
- Wall Street also reacted. While there had been rumors for some time that the bottling company might go public, the sudden social mission of the company caused concerns, and

the investment bankers previously courting the company now cooled off until they could see if the company's retooling would be successful.

The public relations team did exactly what the CEO wanted: generate a lot of publicity about this new product launch. But the publicity also had negative ramifications that could have been avoided.

Avoiding Costly Lawsuits

At the end of the day, most companies view the legal department as a cost center. Legal departments usually put out fires and solve problems, and they are rarely involved in value-creation or revenue-generating activities. All too often, lawyers are sought out late in the process when they have limited ability to be proactively involved in value creation.

At Emerson Jones, the story was no different. As the problems developed, legal became involved to manage the extensive budgets of outside attorneys to litigate the lawsuits, respond to FTC investigations, handle labor disputes, and the like. All of this cost millions of dollars and used up reserves to settle cases. To make matters worse, the cost of prosecuting and maintaining the patents originally sought used up most of the law department's annual budget. This required budgets to be tapped elsewhere in the company to cover these unexpected and unbudgeted legal costs.

Return on Investment

At the end of the project, finance was called upon to evaluate the return on investment. While they had been involved during the capitalization phase and felt strongly about their projections, they were unaware of the looming lawsuits that would destroy the anticipated margin, as well as the spiraling costs of marketing to reinvent the company after the dilution of the name in the marketplace. Investment bankers were no longer interested in taking the company public. They were not prepared for the extensive costs of protecting the many patents that had been filed globally.

To make matters worse, the social goal of Emerson Jones to create a product line consumers would touch and feel and to create an emotional connection to the environment was shoved in a wall where they would never see it, touch it, or feel it. Consumers rarely bought insulation. Maybe if they were building a home or remodeling a home—but it wasn't something they would interact with every day like the villagers in South America who had spawned the idea for the company's shift. And since every other insulation company now boasted the green insulation, no one would ever realize that their insulation was the insulation from Emerson Jones—the one-time bottling company giant that set out to change the world.

Each department and group had been successful in its own right, but the collective end game was wasted time, wasted resources, and failure to achieve the goal.

Although Emerson Jones found itself in a whole lot of trouble, help is on the way. A new way of thinking is emerging. A few of our experts weighed in on the importance of evolving toward the use of multidisciplinary teams and thinking about intellectual property sooner, and they shared some of their success stories.

> I believe deeply that lawyers need to be business people first and lawyers second to deliver value and become a part of the business process. Historically in many organizations, lawyers are seen as a roadblock or someone to just say "no." I believe that forward-thinking businesses want their lawyers to step up and be a part of providing solutions and adding innovative thinking to the goals of the business. I tell the lawyers in our department they aren't allowed to come to a meeting and only say "no," they have to come to the meeting with ideas and solutions.
>
> By conveying a shared vision of working toward common goals and empowering lawyers to think outside the box, I think the result is far more powerful and effective. My goal is that our company leadership views our legal department as a group of savvy business executives who just happen to be lawyers.
>
> A.B. Cruz III,
> Executive Vice President, Chief Legal Officer, and
> Corporate Secretary, Scripps Networks Interactive, Inc.

We have adopted a culture of embracing failure and learning from it and also failing fast. This allows us to explore ideas without fear of repercussions. This type of leadership makes all the difference.

JACQUELINE LEIMER,
Distinguished IP Practitioner, Chicago-Kent College of Law,
Former VP and Associate General Counsel, Kraft Foods,
Former President, International Trademark Association

Innovation doesn't live in one function.

HEIDI EMANUEL,
Senior Innovation Officer, General Mills

We are involved early in the process, often even at the stage of naming a new product or service. We get involved with the naming or branding agency to provide another layer of valuable thinking. I have worked hard to build the relationships and trust to show that I'm not just someone to say "no" or a roadblock. The savvy chief marketing officers understand that we are there to help make the campaign better, build a stronger brand, and ensure that mistakes are not made that lead to litigation.

RUBY ZEFO,
Director, Trademarks and Brands, Intel

Multidisciplinary teams are something that evolved inside P&G in recent years. We were very much structured in silos for many years, as were most other businesses. During that time, the relationships we formed outside of our "silos" or departments was primarily up to us. But I think the people who were really successful understood the importance of reaching outside their department. Instinctively, I always understood that by working as a team we would get our work done better and faster. Those relationships, though, were largely up to us in the earlier days. We had to reach out and form the relationships with other departments, but I always found that's what brought the most success. Now there is more being done to facilitate and encourage those types of relationships and that's a really positive thing for companies and for consumers.

BOB WEHLING,
Former Global Marketing Office, Procter & Gamble

> Failure is the only opportunity to try again more intelligently.
>
> HENRY FORD

Chapter Highlights

- In this chapter, we introduced a case study of a second-generation plastic bottling company plagued with the social conscience of realizing that they are contributing to the erosion of the environment. Determined to turn things around, the CEO charged the company leadership with a new form of recycling: to create a product line that consumers will want and demand to build an emotional connection to the recycling process. He believed that if consumers could touch and feel that recycling was really about reusing resources in a tangible way, they would be more excited about recycling and begin to create a cultural shift. As a second-generation company, the team set out in a linear, black box approach to solving the problem.
- If any ideas are discussed or shared during research and development with outside parties, a nondisclosure agreement must be in place to protect whatever trade secrets are being developed by the company. Any discussion without a nondisclosure agreement will destroy the ability to claim trade secret protection. In many instances, processes and know-how are protected by trade secret law: The Kentucky Fried Chicken secret recipe and the Coke secret ingredient are great examples.
- The cost to globally apply for, protect, and maintain patents may often outweigh the potential return.
- Colors of a product, if unique and distinctive, can be protected. It is essential to ensure that trademark lawyers are aware of all aspects of a product, its packaging and design, in order to protect all aspects of it. Failure to do so means it may be copied and diluted in the marketplace.
- Original music should be copyrighted and protected globally in order to prosecute counterfeiting and copiers in any form.
- Celebrities have rights of publicity in their name and likeness, including the sound of their voice. If you mimic a celebrity, unless it is very clearly in a parody, which is protected by free

speech rights, your company could be exposed to liability for violating rights of publicity.

- Original characters can be a powerful marketing tool and can also be protected by trademark and copyright law.
- The Federal Trade Commission regulates advertising and online marketing to children with stringent regulations that must be followed. Failure to do so can result in significant fines and additional costs in redoing all of the advertising that was at issue.
- If you invest heavily in a consumer education or marketing plan, be mindful that if each component of that campaign is not protected, your competitors will leverage your investment and make it their own.
- Public relations is a critical component of any business. It can generate a lot of attention without the hard cost of advertising and provide credibility and support for key strategic initiatives of the company. If operating in a black box, however, the public relations team may not have the necessary information to determine what is appropriate for release. In our case study, releasing information about the green color of the insulation without the appropriate protections allowed competitors to quickly capitalize on the idea. Further, an innocent statement and quote from R&D unintentionally released important trade secrets of the company. Finally, the news release alerted the labor union to upcoming shifts, creating potential labor problems.
- At the end of our case study, each department had performed brilliantly as independent groups. Because they failed to communicate with one another at critical times, however, the result was a series of costly lawsuits, reinvestment to redo much of the ad campaign that infringed on other rights, the dilution of the critical components of their branding campaign, and the ultimate realization that the product itself was not meeting the social goal of the company. Working as a team, sharing ideas, and communicating throughout the process would have eliminated these problems. At a minimum, it would have reduced costs, eliminated the wasted resources, and increased the likelihood of success.
- Our thought leaders chimed in with a deep understanding of how and why the black box has survived and a call to action that collaboration among subject matter experts is required to thrive.

CHAPTER 6

Integrating a Brand Rewired Process

It's time for a do-over for Emerson Jones. By integrating a Brand Rewired process, the Emerson Jones company will reduce costs, increase turn-around time, and have a greater likelihood of success in its innovation goal. Considering intellectual property issues earlier in the process is critical to success. But to do so requires that a multidisciplinary team approach be implemented in the company. This is not an easy thing to do. Changing cultural norms and the status quo can take a significant dollar and time investment. The key to this increased likelihood of success is three steps:

1. The CEO must demonstrate leadership to create a shared vision and foster the collaboration needed to achieve the shared vision.
2. The CEO must create incentives, financial and/or recognition, for working in a collaborative manner and achieving success.
3. The CEO must implement a process that will facilitate multidisciplinary teams in thinking about how they intersect their creative development process with intellectual property strategy from the beginning.

Emerson creates a team of his top leaders and determines that he will select a facilitator to assist them in working as a team toward his vision. He clearly sets the tone with his leadership team that they are to work in round-table discussions about how to accomplish the goals he has set out.

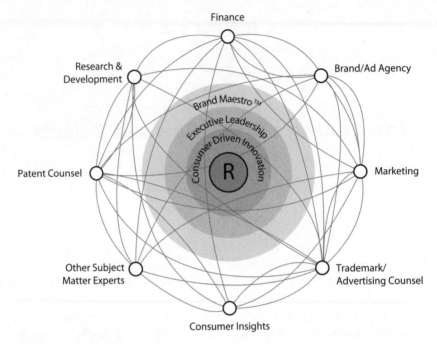

Finance

Research &
Development

Brand/Ad Agency

Brand Maestro ™

Executive Leadership

Consumer Driven Innovation

R

Patent Counsel

Marketing

Other Subject
Matter Experts

Trademark/
Advertising Counsel

Consumer Insights

Figure 6.1   Brand Rewired

As shown in Figure 6.1, which was introduced previously, the company has its leadership and shared vision and is now ready to move forward.

The Environment and Incentives

Armed with buy-in from the company's leadership, the team wanted the new product launch to be a success story. Tapping into the strength of the team, the CEO appointed a Brand Maestro from its ranks. The Brand Maestro would facilitate an innovation session to develop the winning idea and then implement ongoing collaboration-based management with a keen eye on intellectual property strategy to ensure success in the execution of the plan.

The Brand Maestro would require that the team leaders dedicate five days over the next month to proceed through an innovation process designed to cultivate an innovative new solution to achieve the CEO's goal. To set the right environment and atmosphere, the Brand Maestro selected an off-site location designed to foster creativity and collaboration. Selecting an off-site location is important to break down old ways of thinking, remove typical barriers, and allow creativity and collaboration to thrive.

Additionally, the Brand Maestro advised the CEO to create financial and recognition-based incentives for collaboration and teamwork. To break down long-standing stereotypes, fiefdoms, and black boxes, there must be clear leadership and clear incentives. The team was offered profit-sharing bonuses if they were able to achieve the return on investment goal. This bonus would only be provided if the company achieved the desired return on investment, creating an entrepreneurial spirit and team attitude among the corporate leaders.

The Innovation Process

While much of the innovation process mirrors typical tried and true strategic planning and management techniques, the Brand Maestro must follow a proven process to generate the right idea based upon sound thinking and information. The new twist for the Brand Maestro, however, is to bring to the forefront thinking about intellectual property and engage leaders from multiple disciplines in the innovation process.

Day One

The Brand Maestro arrived ready to lead the discussion. The Brand Maestro worked to ensure participation by all. The number one rule of the day—no idea was a bad one. Nothing that anyone contributed was without merit or irrelevant. In fact, it is often the random, outside-the-box stream of consciousness that may lead to the idea that makes the difference. The first day followed fairly typical strategic planning techniques to set the stage for the discussion and provide important background information. While tedious for some, reviewing this information is critical to ensure that all of the team members are working from the same knowledge base.

- Identification of the problem and opportunity
- Review of internal resources available
  - Strengths and weaknesses
- External factors influencing the company
  - Government/regulations
  - Economy/access to capital

- Cultural/societal
- Technological
- Competitive analysis
  - Who are the traditional competitors?
  - Who are nontraditional or indirect competitors?
- Market analysis and consumer insights
  - Who are the stakeholders?
  - What do they want and need and why?
  - What is their daily experience like?
  - How do we know?

Day Two

- Goal setting—what will represent success in quantitative and qualitative means to everyone at the table? By understanding what success means to each discipline, a cohesive and better idea can be formed. What is required to achieve success?
  - R&D
  - Finance, which includes the all-important return on investment analysis
  - Marketing
  - Consumer insights
  - Legal
  - Intellectual asset management and strategy
  - Public relations
  - Human resources

Note that a couple of new departments are involved in the Brand Rewired process. Intellectual asset management and strategy is a group whose primary mission is to ensure that the intellectual assets created in the process are protected and exploited fully. Human resources is added to provide the necessary support and assistance as the multidisciplinary teams take shape, and training and development is needed to reinforce those themes. Introducing these two teams to the discussion can have a profound impact on the outcome.

Day Three

The company had done its background thinking. Everyone had a chance to convey what was important to them and what success meant to them. It was time to start generating ideas. The company added a few other innovation experts to the discussion to help fuel the creative process.

While some in the room might not have considered themselves creative, their presence was equally important. They had a unique skill set and knowledge base that would be needed, and their understanding of how the idea formed was important to their ability to review and analyze how to go forward.

The Brand Maestro again set a golden rule: No idea was bad. No one could say what was wrong with it—even if it was clearly not going to work, in their mind. Sometimes ideas that are fraught with problems can evolve into the right answer if they are given time to percolate. The Brand Maestro reminded the team of a famous Albert Einstein quote.

> I think and think for months and years.
> Ninety-nine times, the conclusion is false.
> The hundredth time I am right.
>
> ALBERT EINSTEIN

The Brand Maestro facilitated a brainstorming session by recalling what had been discussed in the last two days, asking probing questions, and engaging everyone at the table. Ideas were posted up on boards and evolved throughout the day. As ideas were considered, key questions were asked:

Is it compelling?

Is it unique?

Who else is doing something similar?

Why would a consumer buy it?

Can it be protected globally?

Can it be counterfeited easily?

Will it result in lawsuits?

How will we value it?

How will consumers value it?

How will consumers touch, feel, and integrate it into their daily life?

What else might a consumer buy instead?

Can it be done?

How will it be done?

At the end of the day, the team had generated five to seven ideas that could accomplish the goal. The team was then sent out for the next two weeks to do their homework.

Homework—Two Weeks

Each department was to go back and research the ideas discussed for feasibility and likelihood of success from their respective roles. They were to carefully evaluate the ideas and dive deep into the research that was needed from their expert perspectives to determine the ideas' viability. Then they were to come back with recommendations that had the greatest likelihood of success. If none of the ideas met their criteria, that was okay too.

Day Four (after the Two-Week Homework Break)

This fourth day was an important day in the process. The group had been coming together to create what would be, they hoped, the future-of-the-company idea. The Brand Maestro set the tone by reviewing the goals that were set out and the importance of everyone working together, citing the strengths everyone brought to the table. Each department reported on their findings for the ideas based upon pros and cons for each idea. Through continued discussion, probing, and exploration, at the end of the day, the ideas were narrowed to the top three.

Homework—Two Weeks

Each department was given an additional two weeks to further research what would be required to implement the idea from its unique subject matter perspectives. What would achieve the success goals set out? What were their concerns that needed to be addressed in the process? How could they add value to what had already been discovered?

Day Five (after the Two-Week Homework Break)

Day Five was scheduled as the last day of the planning sessions, though more would be added to the schedule if needed to continue the in-depth discussions required for something of this magnitude. The Brand Maestro started by reinforcing the goals of the company and stating the key issues for discussion.

Each department reported its findings and shared any value-added ideas to be considered. The Brand Maestro facilitated the discussion throughout the day to further brainstorm, aggregate, recap, and pose questions to the team. At the end of the day, the CEO and his team had agreed on one final idea that they believed would achieve the company goals. The CEO green-lighted the idea, and now each team had to move into swift action, developing a more detailed plan for execution. But this was not the end of the team meetings. In fact, it was just the beginning. The meetings must become a part of the culture and expected activity to be successful. And so the team moved into implementation.

Implementation

The Brand Maestro would continue to facilitate meetings twice a month during the early implementation phases and then monthly thereafter with a streamlined team of people. The agenda would always be the same:

- Review goals of the project
  - Company goals
  - Group goals
- Intellectual property exploitation and protection
- Time constraints, deadlines
- New issues impacting the launch
- Report by all team leaders on their progress, new issues, or concerns
  - Identification of any issues based upon each report for group discussion
  - Group discussion to bring resolution or determine further homework needed to make better decision on any issues identified
- Celebration of successes achieved
- Identification of new opportunities discovered
- Next steps and benchmarks of success for next meeting

The Brand Maestro served as the expert facilitator with a broad base of knowledge, but with an emphasis in intellectual property strategy, to draw into the discussion the various players when appropriate. The outcome was a cultural phenomenon with an impact far greater than the CEO had imagined.

A Do-Over for Emerson Jones

Working as a team, Emerson Jones determined that recycled plastics could be made into a wide range of products. The finance and R&D team determined that a few key categories were the most cost effective for retooling their existing facility in order to recoup their costs. Through the process, the group determined that to really connect with consumers on a day-to-day basis, they needed something consumers would use every day. After careful consideration and weighing of consumer insights, they decided a line of clothing would provide the most impact to consumers of all ages on a day-to-day basis and would produce a higher margin than anticipated. They could enter into joint-venture agreements with well-known designers who cared about the environment to create lines of clothing for kids and adults that centered on the environmentally friendly tale of a bottling plant turned fashion company.

The name of the product line would be Rebottled. Rebottled was completely clear as a trademark, and they would quickly trademark it in all categories related to fashion, clothing, and accessories. They would dominate the marketplace with this brand. The company would start by targeting their fashions to the average-income household, but hoped to build enough momentum that they could later launch a high-end version of their brand with even higher margins. They determined they must create something iconic about their product line—a symbol like those of Louis Vuitton, Coach, Chanel, and the like. They worked with the top design firms in the country to create a unique iconic symbol for the brand, which would be immediately protected throughout the globe in all categories of fashion. With great inspiration, they also determined that their signature blue color would be used on all the lining, on the soles of shoes, and on the tags in the clothing. Blue like Mother Earth would symbolize Rebottled clothing. The company also quickly protected their now iconic symbol and color.

Rather than pay the high price of a well-known musician, they would hire an up-and-coming, hip band to record an entire album just for them, which they could sell for $1 with the product line and donate the proceeds to sustainability efforts. They would copyright and protect all of those songs and turn one of them into "The Rebottled Song." Once it was protected, they could stop other companies from performing variations of the song. The campaign turned out to be a huge success. Consumers connected with the clothing line not just because it was fashionable, but because they were doing their part to reuse everything in their life. It became a badge of honor to wear the coat with the blue lining or the shoe with the blue sole. The Rebottled designers also went to work to design a new shape of bag that was so unique and distinctive, with a blue lining, of course, that they were able to trademark the design of the bag itself. And the music they hired that up-and-coming band to perform became the most popular music on iTunes and turned the band into a hot commodity. Because of the contracts in place, Emerson Jones found a new source of licensing revenue with an ongoing royalty for the original music they now owned.

Emerson Jones partnered with other fashion companies to reduce its own costs and form valuable partnerships. With strong nondisclosure agreements and joint venture agreements in place, long-lasting business relationships were formed with a mutual interest in protecting the secret processes used by Emerson Jones in making the fibers that turned into Rebottled clothes. Without the extensive patent costs, Emerson Jones redirected its funds into education campaigns about supporting the environment.

When the PR department went to work, they carefully worked with the entire team to deliver a message that showcased the company's social mission without diluting any of its intellectual assets. When the investment bankers arrived and ran their valuation, the brand that had been created and the strength of the intellectual assets that supported that brand had reached the billion-dollar mark. The company was ready to go public, and Emerson Jones had achieved his mission.

At the end of the day, by working as a team, by thinking about how to protect every aspect of what the company was doing, the turn-around time was faster, it cost less, and the likelihood of success was far greater.

The Leadership

Central to the success of the Emerson Jones was the CEO's leadership. The CEO set the tone, had the vision, and invested in the culture to ensure that the group could work as a team and design in strategic creative, innovative, and intellectual property–based thinking to launch a successful new product. It is worth repeating: The CEO knew that to be successful with his mission, he had to do the following:

- Be a leader—create a clear and concise message that builds a shared vision and culture to foster collaboration and teamwork to achieve the common goal.
- Create incentives to overcome years of doing it a different way.
- Support the processes needed to facilitate teamwork and collaboration.

Leaders at all levels of an organization must recognize that these three components are necessary to accomplish any type of organizational change to think about these important issues in a new way. How people are given incentives inside a company and rewarded is critical to successful innovation. The leadership must define success and build in rewards for working collaboratively.

A few of our experts have weighed in with advice and insights on the importance of cultural changes to indoctrinate multidisciplinary thinking.

You can't learn from experiences you aren't having.

BILL THIEMANN,
Executive Vice President, and
BENTON SAUER,
Vice President of Innovation, LPK

I often find that if two people from different disciplines don't agree, then it is all the more important that they keep talking until they do agree. They each have valuable information and we need to facilitate a productive discussion to incorporate what they are both thinking into the solution.

BOB WEHLING,
Former Global Marketing Officer, Procter & Gamble

In building teams within a company, a formal process can be helpful, requiring approval of various groups or departments, but even more important is the informal work that must be done to build strong relationships. Decades ago, executives grew up inside companies so that by the time they were at a high level of leadership, they had formed long-standing relationships with the other executives in the company (and with the trademark attorneys!), making it much easier for that cross-disciplinary discussion and thinking to occur. Today, that doesn't exist in most companies. Now, we all have to work a little harder to build the relationships, form the trust, and respect that we all bring something valuable to the table. The more the culture and leadership can support the formal and the informal processes, the greater the chance of success.

DAVID STIMSON,
Chief Trademark Counsel, Kodak, and
Former President, International Trademark Association

At Northlich, we've put into practice the philosophy that it takes a village to inspire great creative. That's why we're literally organized into client-centric business units that we call "Villages" because they're cross-functional—combining every talent from copywriting to digital to brand strategy—in order to foster ultimate collaboration and idea-sharing.

The great side effect of this is what we call "knowledge accidents." Those are the "aha" moments that are most likely to occur when people from multiple backgrounds get together and share their unique knowledge sets and points of view. These moments cannot occur when everyone works in silos or independently. The creative results have been amazingly powerful for us.

KATHY SELKER,
President, Northlich

An important part of any innovation campaign is to ensure there is cultural support for it. At Kraft Foods, Irene Rosenfeld, our CEO, believes passionately in the need for innovation at all levels of the company, recognizing it can come from anywhere. Kraft Foods company-wide trumpeted "Make Today Delicious." In the R&D or innovation group, we took it a step further to "We invent delicious," so that at all levels of the company, we were thinking about how we invent and innovate to deliver what our consumers want. This is important to build a culture that fosters innovation.

Steve Goers,
Vice President, Open Innovation, Kraft Foods

I make a conscious effort to meet with the chief marketing officer on a regular basis just to touch base and know what's going on, what's on the horizon, and collaborate so we can help each other work toward the common goals of the company. It's essential to take the initiative to meet with people outside your group and be proactive about working as a team.

Ruby Zefo,
Director, Trademarks and Brands, Intel

> If there's nobody in your way, it's because you're not going anywhere.
>
> Robert F. Kennedy

Chapter Highlights

- To introduce the use of multidisciplinary teams and thinking into an organization that was long managed by a linear silo process, it is essential that the cultural shift is driven by leadership creating a shared vision throughout the company of the importance of working in a collaborative team.
- Financial and recognition incentives are critical to changing old ways of thinking. If teams were historically rewarded for working in silos, now they must be rewarded for working in teams. Some form of profit sharing or success sharing financially must be incorporated for company leaders to follow through on what is required.
- Facilitating multidisciplinary teams is not any easy task. Training or developing a Brand Maestro skilled at understanding the many facets that will impact the roll-out of a new product or brand or the reinforcement of an existing brand, including at the forefront intellectual property strategy,

will make the difference between a successful team and an unsuccessful team.

- A carefully structured innovation planning process designed to facilitate involvement by all parties, fostering creative and outside-the-box thinking, with clearly set rules to eliminate stifling attitudes will set the team on a path to achieve successful ideas in a faster turnaround time. By involving all of the key decision makers or stakeholders in the company, there is buy-in and investment in the outcome with a shared sense of ownership and vision.

- As the idea is formed and moves into implementation, regular team meetings are essential to ensure that everyone has the opportunity to weigh in on threats and opportunities, as well as bring value-added thinking.

- Our case study continued through this process, now creating a better idea that would become a cultural phenomenon.

- Our thought leaders weighed in heavily on the need for leadership and cultural changes to embrace multidisciplinary teams in most organizations. While those companies formed in the last 10 years or so may find this an easier philosophy to indoctrinate, those that have been around for more than a hundred years face more challenges. All of our thought leaders agree that multidisciplinary teams and thinking are essential to launching a better brand campaign.

CHAPTER 7

The Brand Maestro

The Brand Maestro is the intellectual property strategy, multi-disciplinary expert within an organization with the unique skill set to facilitate group communication and tap into the strength of various subject matter experts while cohesively executing an innovation or branding plan.

The Brand Maestro must be someone trained in intellectual property strategy, branding, consumer insights, and research and development, but also having skills as a strong process-oriented facilitator. The ability to lead discussion, bring in leadership at key times, be empowered by leadership to do so, be able to maintain and track progress and reinforce incentives for team-based success will be important skills for the Brand Maestro.

In most companies this function may be performed by many different executives: chief marketing officer, chief innovation officer, external business development, chief intellectual property officer, human resource director, or other executives in the company. Whatever the case, an executive must emerge with a unique skill set to cross over these many disciplines.

Additionally, the leadership of the company must recognize the cultural changes needed to embrace a multidisciplinary team and a collaboration approach that designs intellectual property strategy into every aspect of the innovation and branding process. Constant reinforcement of the message, incentives that reinforce this philosophy, and investment in the tools, resources, training, and development are all critical to success.

A Brand Maestro is just the beginning. Without the support of executive leadership, the Brand Maestro will fail. Leaders must carefully consider how they support, foster, and indoctrinate this new way of thinking into their organization.

The Brand Maestro Job Description

The Brand Maestro is an executive leader responsible for the execution of branding and innovation plans to maximize return on investment while building powerful intellectual asset portfolios for the company. The Brand Maestro delivers a brand-based intellectual property strategy for the company. The Brand Maestro will possess a working understanding and knowledge of finance, marketing, intellectual property, risk management, consumer insights, corporate culture management, and group communication.

The Brand Maestro will be skilled and adept at understanding not only how to build a powerful brand and the many creative aspects required to do so, but how to build a powerful intellectual property strategy. While many companies have viewed an intellectual asset strategy as a form that the lawyers complete about what and how they are doing their work, a true intellectual property strategy must incorporate a comprehensive connection to the business strategy.

The Intellectual Asset Strategy

The guiding plan used by the Brand Maestro is an intellectual asset strategy. The intellectual asset strategy encompasses all aspects of how new ideas, innovation, and brands come together to create long-term value for the company. While there are many separate plans to be developed by other team members, a strong, cohesive intellectual asset strategy crossing boundaries is important to achieving long-term success.

An intellectual asset strategy is a plan for a company to use its intellectual assets as important capital assets that will generate revenue, minimize risk or exposure to lawsuits, as well as build long-term value for the company in the event of a spinoff, sale, or merger. Like any strategy, it is a plan to achieve an end-game goal.

To prepare an intellectual property strategy, the Brand Maestro analyzes the company's plans for growth in the development of products and services, its marketing and branding plans, along with a deep understanding of what competitors are doing. The Maestro then backs into what is happening in the creation of intellectual property and modifies company policies and processes to create intellectual assets that further company goals.

For many years intellectual property strategy was considered more of a "clearance" of ideas by lawyers rather than an active part of the company's leadership plans and vision for its future. For a variety of reasons and trends, leading companies view the strategic creation of intellectual assets as equally important as any other part of the overall business plan.

A few key areas that will be incorporated into an intellectual property strategy include the following:

- *Research and Development of New Products and Services.* As products and services are developed by your R&D department, the inevitable question will be asked, "Do we patent, where do we patent, or do we protect this with trade secret law, and what would be required?" Effective intellectual property strategy carefully evaluates how the new product or service will fit into the company's overall strategy and long-term plans, the value of the patent or trade secret in generating revenue, capturing market share, adding value, or exposing the company to risk. As the costs of protecting patents and intellectual assets globally have increased astronomically, so too has the ease of reverse engineering and misappropriation of the same technology. Intellectual property strategists must evaluate the cost benefit of pursuing patents globally versus other means of protecting new products and services. Failure to do so can result in hundreds of millions of wasted dollars spent pursuing something that may ultimately have limited value. Many companies have come to recognize that they have large portfolios of largely unused patents. Many companies are thus spending millions of dollars to maintain patents that are not producing any return.
- *Branding and Marketing.* For many companies, the brand equity they create may be more powerful and last longer than any patents in their portfolio, many of which are outdated before issued. A powerful brand can last forever and evolve with its loyal consumers. Likewise, so can a powerful trademark. A quick search of the trademark database produces millions

of trademarks that have limited to no commercial value or brand equity, diluting the value of what could otherwise become a powerful brand. Marketers and branding experts must consider whether the brand they are creating can be protected. Further, as content and entertainment become a critical part of marketing campaigns, much like soap operas were created to promote soap, the need to copyright and protect all aspects of a campaign is growing. More than just running a "clearance" search to ensure no one else is using a trademark, a strong intellectual property strategy evaluates what makes a strong trademark and can add value to the company's end game.

- *Risk Management.* Risk management continues to be an important part of intellectual property strategy. As lawsuits become more and more prevalent and the cost of intellectual property lawsuits remains one of the highest in the business, companies must carefully evaluate if they will infringe on the rights of others and work proactively rather than reactively to avoid these lawsuits. Involving attorneys with an understanding of intellectual property strategy early in the process can help to avoid these costly lawsuits. All too often, lawyers are brought in at the end of a development process when the subject matter experts are already attached to their ideas. This limits a lawyer's ability to add value or provide important insight, thus diminishing the end result for the company in the creation of intellectual assets.

- *Revenue Generation.* Most importantly, intellectual assets must be evaluated for their ability to generate revenue for the company at the outset. Whether the intellectual asset can result in direct-to-consumer sales, create a market differentiator that will increase revenue, or create an opportunity to partner with others in the supply chain through a joint venture or licensing arrangement, intellectual assets can be an important revenue generator.

- *Improving the Valuation.* Finally, the valuation of intellectual assets has grown dramatically in the last 10 years. As product lines are spun off or sold or the company merges with another, the valuation of intellectual assets becomes an important part of the due diligence and overall valuation. If thought is given in the process of intellectual property creation to how it is ultimately valued, then the likelihood of creating a valuable intellectual property portfolio increases dramatically. This includes considering the impact of dilution and counterfeiting and developing plans to counteract these negative influences.

While the executive team may provide leadership, research and development, patent lawyers, marketing, and trademark lawyers may be acting without active collaboration to maximize results. As has been discussed at length in recent business literature, open innovation and collaboration are critical parts of product development and meaningful innovation. Important questions are asked as a team in a collaborative environment: How will the new products or services be commercialized? How will they be marketed? How will they be sold? Pulling together a team of people that can evaluate all aspects of the product launch life cycle from concept to sales will yield more effective results. A dream intellectual property team would include:

- Brand Maestro—the expert facilitator to lead discussions, create a culture of collaboration and foster teamwork with a deep understanding of strategic planning at all levels.
- Finance—the experts who will understand how the company finances its endeavors, what is needed to achieve the desired return on investment, and how the development will result in positive or negative changes in the annual valuation, as well as in contemplated future merger and acquisition activity.
- R&D—the experts in your company's burgeoning products or services, the technicians who know what needs to be done to make it work and how to make it work.
- Patent lawyers—the experts who will evaluate the patentability of the products and provide important freedom to practice opinions on what else is out there.
- Business development—the leaders creating new opportunities and business relationships.
- Sales—the salesperson on the front lines knows what your competitors are doing, has knowledge of what consumers want, and can add important perspective to whether what is being developed can be sold.
- Marketing and branding—the experts who will take the product or service you have and develop the campaign around it.

This includes everything from product packaging, naming and branding, distribution, to the campaign that will connect with its consumers.

- Trademark/trade dress—the experts who will evaluate what aspects of the campaign can be protected. What adds value is participating in the process so that not only is it something that has some level of protection, but it is a powerful trademark or trade dress that can provide the most powerful protection globally.
- Intellectual property strategy experts—the expert attorneys or consultants with a broad base of knowledge who can evaluate how it all comes together to meet the company goals and achieve the end-game results in a valuable intellectual asset portfolio, as well as to protect the intellectual assets of the company globally.

At Kraft Foods, we recently created an IP strategy team whose specific function is to work within the research and development group to identify what has potential as an intellectual asset for the company, and then build a plan as it moves out of R&D and goes to legal, marketing, and so on. They are an important part of the Idea2 Market process that is designed to maximize the use of a collaborative team through the innovation life cycle.

JACQUELINE LEIMER,
Distinguished IP Practitioner, Chicago-Kent College of Law,
Former VP and Associate General Counsel, Kraft Foods,
Former President, International Trademark Association

The Brand Maestro will work with the team to create and continually develop an intellectual asset strategy based upon various business groups, projects, or other categorization. The general components of an intellectual property strategy will include:

Objectives—What is the objective of the intellectual asset/project?

Measurement Tools—How will success be defined? When will it be measured?

Strategies—What will be done, why, by whom, and by when?

Development—How will the brand and IP be created and tested?

Exploitation—How will the IP be fully leveraged in the marketplace?

Risk Management—How will lawsuits and risk be avoided?

Enforcement—How will the IP be protected?

Tactics—What are the details of how it will get done?

Incentives—How are team members provided incentives to work collaboratively?

Return on Investment—What is the project cash and revenue impact to the company or anticipated return on investment?

An intellectual property strategy must be created and understood at multiple levels of a company. At a high level and from the top of the company, the role intellectual property will play in driving or supporting the company's overall business strategy must be defined and actively managed by the business. From that high level understanding, more specific business strategies, IP strategies, and IP tactics can be formulated and implemented for each project within the company to deliver on the core business strategies. That alignment between intellectual property and strategy and overall corporate mission is critical to success.

INGER ECKERT,
Chief Counsel, Intellectual Property,
International Paper Company

When we build an intellectual property strategy we are focused on the following:

- Selection of the best possible brands (the overall product and consumer experience)
- Protection of those brands
- Enforcement globally

To really be effective we need to be involved as early as possible in the creative process to provide guidance as to what will give us the most bang for our buck. Focus groups may not always have the right answers. We find that when a focus group is given options of a name for a new product, they will often pick the one that is most descriptive. It's human nature to pick something that describes the product because that's easier to understand, when, in fact, the most powerful brands are the arbitrary ones that through a variety of marketing efforts, become inextricably linked in the minds of the public with the products on which they are used. As a result, our job is to help marketers understand that by creating unique and arbitrary names or designs for our products and services, we can better protect them globally. If we do our job properly, they quickly realize we have a greater chance at long-term economic success.

Critical to success is leadership support of collaborative teams and a cultural change to embrace a new way of thinking about how we work and what is valued. This is not easy, but can be done with the right leadership and execution.

GREGG MARRAZZO,
Vice President and Chief Counsel,
Intellectual Property and Global Marketing, Kimberly-Clark

How to Get Started in Your Organization

Whether you are an entrepreneurial growing company, a leader in a large global corporation, or work in an agency environment, the principles discussed here can be implemented and incorporated into your organization. If you don't have all of the disciplines needed within your organization, can you tap into those resources externally? Consider your organization and the need for designing intellectual property strategy into your innovation and branding process through multidisciplinary teams. There are a number of steps to consider:

- Evaluate what processes you currently use in creating new products, services, and marketing and branding campaigns and your current brand portfolio.
- Identify the goals your company has for innovation, market leadership, brand development, and short- and long-term goals to maximize return on investment of current and future brands, new technologies, and other intellectual assets.
- Identify your multidisciplinary team.
- Identify a leader or Brand Maestro to serve as the facilitator of the multidisciplinary team.

- Utilize the Brand Rewired key intersection points defined in Chapter 3 to add strategy without stifling creativity.
- Identify what training may be required to utilize a multidisciplinary approach.
- Create the process you will utilize to facilitate discussions when embarking on new projects, as well as the regular monthly meetings to intersect IP strategic thinking during the creative process.
- What tools will you use to document and track the evolution of the ideas and plans developed?
- What agenda will you set for the regular meeting?
- How will you provide incentives to your team to work collaboratively rather than independently?
- How will you set the tone and the message that fosters teamwork across disciplines, that supports the process to be used, and gives your people incentives for working together?
- Audit your existing intellectual asset portfolio and determine what goals and objectives you have for exploitation and protection of that portfolio.

> Never tell people how to do things. Tell them what to do and they will surprise you with their ingenuity.
>
> GENERAL GEORGE S. PATTON, JR.

Chapter Highlights

- Designing intellectual property in the innovation and branding process is a cultural shift for most organization. A clear commitment to this way of thinking from the leadership is essential to achieve buy-in from all stakeholders.
- The Brand Maestro is an executive within the company who possesses a unique skill set centered on facilitation of multidisciplinary teams with a deep understanding of culture management and group decision making. This executive will have expertise in intellectual property strategy and a broad base of knowledge of the areas that impact the development of new ideas: research and development, consumer insights,

marketing and branding, intellectual property, legal and risk management, public relations, and human resources.

- The Brand Maestro will lead a team of subject matter experts in the process of creating and maintaining new products, services, and brands. The dream team includes finance, technology, consumer insights, marketing, legal, and public relations.

- A central function of the Brand Maestro is to build and continuously manage an intellectual property strategy for the company. This will include a careful plan of how the company will develop, exploit, protect, and maximize return on investment of its intellectual assets over the long term.

- If you are ready to get started developing a Brand Rewired program in your company, it is essential to begin by auditing what processes are currently in place and identifying your goals for the future development and management of intellectual assets in your organization. Once you know what you have and what you want, asking and answering a series of questions can rewire the process.

- Leadership setting a vision and giving a clear message that fosters and supports designing in intellectual property strategy, and having multidisciplinary teams are critical to success.

- A process that facilitates collaboration is necessary to help bridge cultural gaps and old ways of thinking.

- Incentives will ensure that your team wants to work toward those common goals.

CHAPTER 8

The Thought Leaders

While most companies have not yet hired a Brand Maestro, the beginnings of a Brand Rewired approach are growing in many leading companies. We overview here just a few of the companies and thought leaders we researched and/or interviewed and provide short excerpts of their approach to collaborative teams. We have sought to interview the leaders in companies that have been established for more than 100 years, as well as those that have recently emerged in the last 10 years, to provide a unique perspective.

General Mills

General Mills traces its roots to two flour mills on the banks of the Mississippi River. Officially formed in a merger of regional flour milling companies in 1928, the stock for the company was first traded on the New York Stock Exchange on November 30, 1928. To assist in its growth, the company maintained a philosophy of allowing the mills to keep their own identity. Several well-known brands and marketing campaigns boosted the company's growth. In 1907, Benjamin S. Bull, ad manager for the Washburn Crosby Company, created an advertising campaign that used the slogan, "Eventually . . . Why Not Now?" This campaign was so popular that it forced then-competitor Pillsbury to create a responsive ad campaign stating "Because Pillsbury's Best." The ad was used well into the 1940s.

Another example of marketing success occurred in 1921, when an advertisement ran in the *Saturday Evening Post* for Gold Medal Flour asking customers to complete and return a jigsaw puzzle to receive a free small pincushion. Unforeseen by the company, some 30,000 of the jigsaw puzzles were returned accompanied by letters asking baking and cooking questions. To assist in answering these letters, a fictional female personality was introduced by the Washburn Crosby Company. In honor of their recently retired director, William Crocker, the company gave this new employee the surname "Crocker," and since they believed this new personality would have to be friendly in answering all of the questions, she was given the amiable first name "Betty." This imaginary employee of General Mills would become—and still remains—one of General Mills' most successful brands, Betty Crocker.

There was another discovery in 1921, when a health clinician in Minneapolis, Minnesota, accidentally spilled bran gruel mix on a hot stove. The gruel mix baked into a crispy flake that the health clinician thought tasted good. Ultimately, this mishap would lead to the creation of one of General Mills' most popular brands, Wheaties. Wheaties was not without its challenges. In fact, the brand was on the brink of discontinuation in 1929, until then ad manager Sam Gale noticed that the "Have You Tried Wheaties?" radio campaign was a success in the markets where it was being used and the company decided to take the campaign national. Then, in 1933, the phrase "Breakfast of Champions" was coined for the first time when the brand began to sponsor baseball radio broadcasts. One of the company's sponsored announcers was voted the most popular Wheaties baseball announcer in 1937, thereby earning him a free trip to California. While there, he auditioned for a screen test and went on to become a Hollywood star and the 40th president of the United States, Ronald Reagan.

The company also aided its growth by diversifying its interests and acquiring other companies. For instance, in 1924, the company purchased failing radio station WLAG and renamed it WCCO—the initials for the Washburn Crosby Company. In 1965, the company purchased Rainbow Crafts, the manufacturer of Play-Doh. In 1970, it entered the restaurant business by purchasing Red Lobster and then others, and later launched the Olive Garden in 1982. Over the years the company has sponsored several television shows, including *The Lone Ranger* from 1949 to 1961 and *The Bullwinkle Show* beginning in 1959. Perhaps the coup de grâce occurred when it acquired longtime competitor Pillsbury in 2001.

Today, General Mills is headquartered in Minneapolis, Minnesota. Thanks to the success of the advertising campaigns just discussed and the creation of some of the most popular brands on the market (including such brands as Cheerios, Green Giant, and Häagen-Dazs), General Mills has grown to become one of America's premier Fortune 500 companies.

> Our innovation process has utilized collaborative teams for many years. As a food company, we are always looking for new ways to expand the reach of our brands rather than traditional research and development to create new products or technologies. When we innovate, we start with the brand architecture, evaluating what it stands for, what it promises, and how its consumers live and interact with the brand. We identify brand boundaries for innovation and then immerse ourselves in the consumer's life to identify new ideas. We innovate based upon consumer needs. In our process, we strive for all comments to provide three positives about a new idea before a negative comment is made about an opportunity or idea to foster innovation through the team approach. This is particularly important when bringing in senior people from varying functions to ensure that no idea is overlooked.
>
> It costs a lot of money to launch a new brand, so we are always interested in attaching related products to existing brands.
>
> HEIDI EMANUEL,
> Senior Innovation Officer, General Mills

Procter & Gamble

Founded in 1837, Procter & Gamble (P&G) has become one of the leading manufacturing companies in the world and a top Fortune 500 company. Headquartered in Cincinnati, Ohio, P&G currently employs over 135,000 people in more than 80 countries. It is ranked sixth on Fortune's "Global Most Admired Companies" list, third on Barron's "World's Most Respected" list, and 12th on *BusinessWeek*'s list of "World's Most Innovative Companies." According to the company itself, one of its many brands touches the lives of people around the world approximately four billion times a day. The company continues to grow, thanks in part to its philosophy of providing products and services of superior quality and value.

P&G is a company rich in history. William Procter, a candle-maker from England, and James Gamble, a soap maker from Ireland, married the Norris sisters. During the Panic of 1837, the husbands began to compete with each other because their industries were pulling from the same resources and clientele. Due to this discord, their father-in-law, Alexander Norris, held a meeting with the two men and convinced them to create a partnership. As a result, Procter & Gamble was formed in October 1837 as a small, family-operated soap and candle company.

By 1859, the company had 80 employees and sales of approximately $1 million. During the Civil War years, the company won the contract to supply the Union Army with soap and candles. This contract led to both increased profits and exposure of its brands to the masses. Then, in 1879, a worker accidentally left the soap machine running while they were at lunch. During the time they were gone, air entered into the soap mixture and created a new kind of floating soap. After experimenting with this product, it was finally perfected into one of P&G's leading brands, Ivory soap.

P&G has repeatedly been a pioneer in innovation throughout its history. In 1887, the company instituted a pioneer program giving employees an ownership stake in the company in an effort to avoid potential strikes in the future. In 1924, P&G became the first company to conduct deliberate data-based market research with consumers in efforts to better understand consumers' actions. In 1941, it was the first company to correspond with consumers through a consumer relations department.

The company's growth was also aided by its branding and advertising campaigns. During the 1920s and 1930s, the company sponsored a number of radio programs that became known as "soap operas" due to the nature of the company's products. This placed the company in the homes of many American consumers on a daily basis. Assisted by this advertising campaign, P&G acquired the Thomas Headley Company from England in 1940. In 1946, one of P&G's most successful brands, Tide, was introduced as a new formula that cleaned better than anything else on the market. In 1955, in a partnership with Indiana University, the company released another of its most successful brands, Crest, which was marketed as the first toothpaste on the market to contain fluoride. In 1957,

P&G purchased Charmin Paper Mills, and in 1961, it introduced Pampers as the first affordable, dependable disposable diaper brand on the market. And, in 2005, P&G purchased Gillette, expanding its brand names to include Gillette razors, Duracell, and Oral-B.

As a result of these innovations and the success of its branding practices, Procter & Gamble boasts of more than 170 years of introducing brands that make life easier for the consumer. Each year, the company sells more than $1 billion worth of 22 different brands. Among the most popular brands today are Head & Shoulders, Ivory soap, Tide, Dawn, Pampers, Gillette, Charmin, and Crest. To ensure the continuation of this success, the company invests more than $7 billion a year in advertising. The company also invests more than $2 billion each yearand has created programs such as Connect and Develop^{SM}, Future Works, and Clay Street to enhance and accelerate innovation.

Connect + Develop

Connect + Develop is one of Procter & Gamble's innovative strategies designed to increase the company's success. Implemented in 2001, Connect and Develop is a process that allows externally developed intellectual property to be brought into P&G and alternatively, permit internally developed assets and know-how to be used by others externally. The purpose of this strategy is to sustain growth moving forward. Under this program, P&G wants to be the preferred partner for open innovation and actively seeks to connect with external partners (both individuals and companies of all sizes) to find the best-in-class-solutions to increase innovation in packaging, marketing models, research methods, engineering, and technology. Since its inception in 2001, more than 50% of P&G's innovation has been sourced externally.

Future Works

FutureWorks is P&G's entrepreneurial new business generator, and a part of Procter & Gamble's Connect + Develop strategy. By connecting with external partners, P&G FutureWorks scope has expanded beyond P&G's strategic core businesses into new channels and domains. P&G FutureWorks seeks to create adjacencies and new business models for brands in high-growth categories. P&G FutureWorks helps transform fledgling companies currently serving new market business into companies that can scale to serve mass markets. FutureWorks strives to create, develop, and discover ideas and partnerships that create thriving new P&G business units and expand their brands into new market segments. An example of a product that has benefited from FutureWorks is the Mr. Clean Car Wash franchise system, whereby the brand Mr. Clean was leveraged with the car wash industry, thereby helping P&G to expand the brand name beyond its typical market.

Clay Street

In 2004, Procter & Gamble began an innovation experiment called "the clay street project." The laboratory is a five-story building, located on Clay Street, in Cincinnati's inner city where multifunctional teams are brought together to solve P&G businesses' most difficult challenges and make a lasting impact on the people and the organization.

The approach centers on a deep understanding of how humans best work together to solve complex problems and achieve breakthrough success. Now, eighteen sessions and almost 200 team members later, the clay street project has repeatedly shown teams how to discover new gifts, make uncommon connections, and reveal their genius. These teams have made a lasting impact throughout P&G by revitalizing troubled brands, delivering breakthrough product innovations, creating new categories, and inspiring culture change. One of the clay street project's earliest and greatest successes has been the restage of Herbal Essence, which became the second-leading hair care brand in the United States. Additional breakthroughs followed, including the launch of Ariel Excel Gel, named "the best laundry detergent ever tested" by *Which?* magazine; and the category-creating launch of SWASH, a new fabric refresher brand aimed at fashion-conscious Gen-Yers. As the clay street project has grown, their core principle has remained unchanged: focus on revealing human potential and amazing innovation will follow.

Marketing research and consumer understanding must drive all innovation.

Within P&G, ideas based upon consumer insights can come from many different places. Ideas that have potential, create a team of people in all disciplines including Consumer Market

Knowledge, Marketing, Product Supply (manufacturing and logistics), Customer Business Development (Sales), IP strategy counsel, and others that can take the project from concept to the marketplace. These become brand-building organizations within the company.

We are always looking for strategies to build a stronger product and/or service and a higher fence of protection around it. We know and practice daily involving the right counsel early in the process. This not only avoids potential issues, but ensures we have the best protection available to outperform competitors.

JEFF WEEDMAN,
Vice President, Global Business
Development, Procter & Gamble

Kraft Foods

In 1903, James L. Kraft started a wholesale door-to-door cheese business in Chicago, Illinois. In its first year of business, Kraft Foods lost $3,000 and a horse. Despite this, the business survived, and Kraft's four brothers joined him to form the JL Kraft & Brothers Company in 1909. By 1914, they were selling 31 different varieties of cheese around the country. The next year, they invented a process to pasteurize cheese, thereby increasing its shelf life and decreasing the need for refrigeration, a process that they patented in 1916.

Kraft Foods began to soar during World War I, when it sold six million pounds of products to the United States Army. Immediately following the war, it began a national advertising campaign and made its first acquisition of another company, the Canadian Cheese Company, in 1919. Following on the success of the last decade, the company changed its name to Kraft Foods Cheese Company and went public in 1924. To sustain its growth, the company purchased the Phenix Cheese Company (to become Kraft Foods-Phenix), the manufacturers of Philadelphia cream cheese. In 1930, Kraft Foods had grown to the point of controlling 40 percent of the United States cheese market. This feat was aided by the fact that the National Dairy Products Corporation (makers of Breyers ice cream and Breakstone cottage cheese and sour cream) purchased Kraft Foods-Phenix the same year. Growth continued to excel in 1933, when the company began marketing by sponsoring radio programs.

During World War II, the company sent approximately four million pounds of cheese a week to Britain to assist in the war effort. In 1945, the company changed its name to Kraft Foods Company. During the 1960s, Kraft Foods continued to expand its product base and went global. In 1976, the name was once again changed to Kraft Foods, Inc., in preparation of continued mergers and acquisitions that would occur throughout the 1980s. Then Phillip Morris Company purchased Kraft Foods in 1988 for $12.9 billion. In 1989, Kraft Foods merged with General Foods, bringing some of the best brands in the food and beverage industry under one umbrella, Kraft Foods General Foods. In 1995, the name once again became Kraft Foods, and on September 22, 2008, Kraft Foods replaced AIG on the Dow Jones Industrial Average.

Kraft Foods (www.kraftfoodscompany.com) makes today delicious in 150 countries around the globe. Its 100,000 employees work tirelessly to make delicious foods consumers can feel good about. From American brand icons like *Kraft* cheeses, dinners, and dressings, *Maxwell House* coffees and *Oscar Mayer* meats, to global powerhouse brands like *Oreo* and *LU* biscuits, *Philadelphia* cream cheeses, *Jacobs* and *Carte Noire* coffees, *Tang* powdered beverages, and *Milka*, *Côte d'Or*, *Lacta*, and *Toblerone* chocolates, its brands deliver millions of smiles every day. Kraft Foods (NYSE: KFT) is the world's second largest food company with 2008 revenues of $42 billion. The company is a member of the Dow Jones Industrial Average, Standard & Poor's 500, the Dow Jones Sustainability Index and the Ethibel Sustainability Index.

> Innovation can mean different things to different people in different frames of reference. In my role at Kraft Foods as the VP of Open Innovation, it comes down to two words:
> *What*
> Consumer insights
> Business strategies
> Create key needs within the company
> *How*
> Do we find solutions internally or externally?
> Do we become smarter about protecting and levering our IP?
> Innovation is always targeted against our brands. Brands are our most powerful asset and most of our innovation occurs within the existing brand framework.

My role is primarily about open innovation, knowledge management, and IP strategy within our core business functions. I focus on building the capabilities, processes and culture change to enable sharing of knowledge internally and accessing external know how and innovation. We can't afford to reinvent the wheel internally, so we need to collaborate and share information more effectively. Likewise, we can't afford not to tap into the external innovation and discovery that occurs outside Kraft Foods. I try to measure how effectively we are innovating at Kraft Foods based upon those three criteria.

Old solutions can be answers to new problems. Our job is to connect the dots.

STEVE GOERS,
Vice President, Open Innovation, Kraft Foods

Kimberly-Clark

Kimberly-Clark is a tale of two successful companies on a path to become one super-company in the paper industry. In 1865, Thomas Seymour Scott and Otis H. Ballou created a partnership to form a wholesale paper business known as Ballou and Scott. This was the beginning of Scott Paper Company in 1874. Scott Paper Company flourished in the early 1900s. In 1907, it introduced the first disposable paper towel to help fight the common cold. In 1913, Scott Paper exceeded the $1 million in sales threshold and began to manufacture ScotTissue, a leading brand of toilet paper. Two years later, it marketed the slogan, "It's the counted sheet that counts," when it become the first to sell toilet paper by the sheet. That same year, Scott Paper went public and joined the New York Stock Exchange.

In 1931, Scott Paper expanded its product line to paper towels in the home with the ScotTowels paper towel roll. This became the country's top-selling paper towel brand. In the 1950s, Scott Paper acquired and merged with several other companies, and it became the first company to produce a nationally televised advertisement for bathroom tissue. In 1972, Scott Paper introduced one of its leading brands, Cottonelle bathroom tissue.

Simultaneously, four businessmen, John Kimberly, Havilah Babcock, Charles B. Clark, and Frank C. Shattuck partnered in Wisconsin and invested $30,000 to form Kimberly, Clark and Company. Originally, this company built the Globe Mill to make newsprint entirely from linen and cotton rags. In 1878, a group of companies including Kimberly, Clark and Company invested to form the Atlas Paper Company, the first company in Wisconsin to produce paper from ground or organic pulp. Among the first products was the new invention of wrapping paper.

Throughout its history, Kimberly, Clark and Company consistently expanded by acquiring or constructing new mills. By 1886, it had become the leading paper producer in the Midwest. The company incorporated in 1906. In 1918, as a result of the First World War, Kimberly, Clark and Company created and produced cellucotton as a substitute for cotton. This material was used as bandages on the front, but later became the source of development for the brands of Kotex (feminine products) and Kleenex (facial tissue).

In 1925, Kimberly, Clark and Company expanded outside the United States and began to market its product in Canada. Several years later, the stock was offered to the public and the company joined the New York Stock Exchange on May 8, 1929. Then, during the Second World War, Kimberly, Clark and Company once again assisted its country and shifted its focus to the production of defense needs, such as anti-aircraft gun mounts and detonating fuses for heavy shells. During this same time, Kimberly, Clark and Company adopted Little Lulu, a cartoon figure in the *Saturday Evening Post*, to help explain the Kleenex shortage during the war. This partnership would last into the 1950s and would ultimately lead to one of the largest advertising signs in Times Square. Also in 1955, the company began a decade of major international expansion by investing in its first non–North American facility. Additionally, during this time, Kimberly, Clark and Company began to develop surgical and health care products. More recently, Kimberly, Clark and Company has produced some of its most well-known brands. For instance, in 1979, the company introduced Huggies disposable diapers. Then, in 1980, the company introduced the Depend line of incontinence care products.

In the mid-1990s, things began to change for both Kimberly and Scott Paper, as they both began to strategize for long-term sustainability. To do this, both began to divest their companies of nonessential businesses and assets. This ultimately led to a $9.4 billion merger between Kimberly, Clark and Company and Scott Paper in 1995. After the merger, Kimberly, Clark and Company introduced a yellow Labrador puppy as its face for the bath tissue brands within its company. This puppy became the first ever brand to earn a place among the celebrity wax figures at Madame Tussaud's in London, England, in 2004.

Today, Kimberly-Clark employs nearly 53,000 people in 37 countries on its way to posting sales of over $19 billion a year. Some of Kimberly-Clark's leading brands include Kleenex, Huggies, Kotex, Depend, Scott, Cottonelle, and Pull-Ups. According to the company, approximately 1.3 billion people use its products every day. The company is headquartered in Irving, Texas.

> In this economic downturn, there will be fewer, but more meaningful investments. The most important investment any company can make is in innovation and brands. At Kimberly-Clark, we are focused on vetting ideas early in the process to ensure they connect with the consumer and the brand promise. If this happens we will produce the necessary return on investment by growing sales and increasing margins.
>
> We have established a cultural shift of understanding that all innovation must stem from customer wants and needs.
> - Define the brand promise by understanding the consumer.
> - Develop the technologies that deliver on that promise.
> - This in turn will create equity.
>
> Previously, ideas might move through the system in a very linear fashion without prioritization of what the consumer really wanted. A lot of money can be wasted if you don't base your innovation decisions on consumer insights.
>
> GREGG MARRAZZO,
> Vice President and Chief Counsel,
> Intellectual Property and Global Marketing, Kimberly-Clark

Kodak

Eastman Kodak Company is a multinational corporation that produces imaging and photographic materials and equipment as consumer and commercial goods.

The company's founder was George Eastman, the man who would ultimately invent roll film and help make everyone a photographer. Mr. Eastman was a high school dropout who was judged "not especially gifted." He dropped out of school in order to provide financial support for his family. While working steady jobs at an insurance company and a local bank, George worked at night on ways to simplify the photography process. After three years of experimentation, he found a working formula.

Kodak is a rare case where the name of the company is its brand. It is purported that the letter "K" was a favorite of Eastman's, because "it seems a strong, incisive sort of letter." It is also purported that the name "Kodak" was developed when he and his mother were playing with an anagram set. Finally, when developing the name "Kodak," Eastman had three things in mind for the name. It needed to be short, it needed to be a name that could not be mispronounced, and it could not resemble anything or be associated with anything but "Kodak."

In 1880, Mr. Eastman leased the third floor of a building on State Street in Rochester, New York, and began to manufacture dry plates for sale to the masses. However, this venture proved costly and nearly put Eastman out of business. After producing a bad batch of dry plates, Eastman recalled the product and replaced the plates, nearly causing both personal and company financial ruin. It is reported that Eastman explained that "making good on those plates took our last dollar. But what we had left was more important—reputation."

Eastman next began to focus on the company's growth. In 1888, Eastman adopted the slogan for Kodak, "You Press the Button, We Do the Rest!" It is also reported he repeatedly stated that his goal was to "make the camera as convenient as the pencil." In this same year, Eastman registered the trademark for Kodak. In the next decade, the word "Kodak" sparkled from an electric sign in London's Trafalgar Square.

As his company continued to prosper, Eastman became more charitable, a trait many attribute to greatly increasing the company's success. In 1919, Eastman gave one-third of his own company holdings, then worth $10 million, to his employees, because he believed they made his company prosper. Also during this time, he established a retirement annuity, life insurance, and a disability benefit plan for his employees. Kodak's headquarters are in Rochester, New York. Today, the company employs nearly 25,000 people.

We have continued to evolve into a company that works to understand the needs of its customers and looks for new market opportunities. Our technology may be ever changing, but the brand and belief in the brand remains the same. This allows us to constantly understand what our customers want and need, create the technology to serve those needs, while always earning and maintaining their trust in the brand.

When I work with the marketing team at Kodak, I focus primarily on understanding the overall objectives and serving as a valuable business advisor to the team. After my 20 years with the company, they know I'm there to bring a unique perspective. We work hard as an interdisciplinary team to identify what brand strategy will best accomplish our shared objectives.

At Kodak, we roll out new products and services constantly, but all under the umbrella of the Kodak master brand. At the forefront of my thinking is how do we ensure that the integrity and value of the brand is maintained. Throughout the creative process we continue to go back to our goal and ask ourselves, will what we are doing strengthen the brand in the long term? The answer must be "Yes."

DAVID STIMSON,
Chief Trademark Counsel, Kodak, and
Former President, International Trademark Association

Harley-Davidson

In 1901, William S. Harley drew a blueprint of an engine designed to fit a bicycle. Two years later, he partnered with Arthur Davidson to produce the first ever Harley-Davidson motorcycle in a 10-by-15-foot wooden shed. The first purchaser was Henry Meyer of Milwaukee, Wisconsin. Then, in 1904, the first Harley-Davidson dealer opened. The Harley-Davidson Motor Company, Inc. was incorporated on September 17, 1907. In 1910, the famous "Bar and Shield" logo was used for the first time and trademarked the next year. As quickly as 1912, within a decade of its founding, the company exported its first product to Japan, beginning its international business.

Throughout its history, Harley-Davidson received notoriety among motorcyclists by consistently having some of the most famed motorcycle racers in the country ride its product. It was also aided through the creation of *The Enthusiast* magazine, which began its reign as the longest continuously published motorcycle magazine in 1916. In the late 1910s and early 1920s, a team of farm boys nicknamed "The Wrecking Crew" consistently won races while riding

Harley-Davidson motorcycles. The group had a pig as a mascot. After each winning race, they would take a victory lap with a real pig (or hog) aboard their Harley motorcycles. At least one journalist noted that team "Harley-Davidson" was "hogging" all of the top positions. This was the first known use of the word "hog" in association with Harley-Davidson. They also marketed the brand through the introduction of black leather motorcycle jackets in 1947.

The two world wars aided in the company's growth. In 1917, nearly one-third of the motorcycles produced were sold to the U.S. military. In 1918, this number increased to nearly half of all those produced. It has been estimated that by war's end, the army used approximately 20,000 motorcycles, most of which were produced by Harley-Davidson. In fact, the Harley-Davidson motorcycle was so prevalent in the war that Corporal Roy Holtz, the first American to enter Germany the day after the armistice was signed, did so riding a Harley bike. Thanks in a large part to the war, Harley-Davidson became the largest motorcycle manufacturer in the world by 1920, having over 2,000 dealers in 67 countries. The company was also aided by World War II, when this time street bike production of the motorcycle was almost entirely halted for military purposes. In fact, in 1943, the company received the first of four Army-Navy "E" awards for excellence in wartime production. This introduced a whole new generation of Americans to the product, something that would benefit Harley-Davidson after the war.

During the 1960s, the company diversified into the manufacturing of golf carts and became the third largest manufacturer of these products. Also in 1969, it merged with American Machine and Foundry Company (AMF). However, this relationship was short-lived, as AMF would not fully commit to their motorcycle business. As a result, 13 senior executives signed a letter of intent to buy Harley-Davidson Motor Company from AMF for $80 million in 1981. Once the buyback was official, the new slogan, "The Eagle Soars Alone," was introduced. In 1983, the Harley Owners Group (H.O.G.) was created, and within six years, its membership reached more than 90,000. By 2000, the group had over 500,000 members. In 1986, the Motor Company was listed on the American Stock Exchange, and in 1987, the New York Stock Exchange. In 1998, the company opened its first operational facility outside the United States, in Brazil. This was a critical time for the company. Through the licensing and protection of its brand, it was able to grow and survive.

The company is headquartered in Milwaukee, Wisconsin. The branding strategy is so successful that licensing of the logo accounts for 5 percent of the company's net revenue each year. Among the company's more successful products are the Sportster, Dyna, Softail, and Touring motorcycles, and the Revolution engine.

> Harley-Davidson for many years operated through tribal knowledge to manage its brand. Everyone knew what the Harley-Davidson brand symbolized and meant to its owners and to the world. As the brand expanded and its value increased we knew we had to take more proactive measures to protect it at all costs. For many years, it was something that was handed down more than written down. In recent years, however, we have recognized that the need to take this asset that we have in our culture and develop processes that extend its value as well as protect the brand. Both are equally important. The brand's values and culture of the company drive the vision and the tone. The application and formalization of, and disciplined application of this new process is what facilitates making it happen in an effective way.
>
> JOANNE BISCHMANN,
> Vice President, Licensing and Special Events, Harley-Davidson

Yahoo!

In 1994, two Stanford University students, Jerry Yang and David Filo, were writing their doctoral theses, when they realized that they had spent much of their time surfing the World Wide Web and cataloging their favorite web sites. Later that same year, the two men launched "Jerry and David's Guide to the World Wide Web," a site that immediately soared in popularity. As the site's notoriety increased, the partners decided to develop a new name. Playing off the phrase "Yet Another Compiler Compiler," the team created "Yet Another Hierarchical Officious Oracle," or Yahoo! The partners are also rumored to have liked the word's definition of "rude, unsophisticated and uncouth."

Under the original domain name of akebono.stanford.edu/yahoo, the site quickly outgrew Stanford's capabilities. On January 18, 1995, the Yahoo! domain name was created. Then, on March 2, 1995, Yahoo! was incorporated. To generate its initial revenue, the company used banner advertising deals, selling space on its web page to other companies that wanted to promote themselves to those who frequent yahoo.com. These banner advertisements would also link the user directly to that company's web site. Also, the company entered into distribution deals with other web sites looking to increase their own Internet traffic, and would then lead the yahoo.com users to that site and receive a cut of any transactions made as a result. Both of these tactics allowed for Yahoo! to offer its services to the public free of charge. On April 12, 1996, the company went public and sold 2.6 million shares at $13 each. By the end of the first day of trading, the stock had soared to $43 per share.

Also in 1996, Yahoo! began focusing on marketing and realized that Yahoo! itself was a brand that needed to be advertised, leading to the launching of the company's first national advertising campaign. As a part of this campaign, the company released a television commercial and created the slogan, "Do You Yahoo?" Another tactic of the advertising campaign was to saturate the market with the logo, so they began placing posters at sporting events, concerts, and so on and printed the logo on Ben & Jerry's ice cream containers and Visa credit cards. An article in *Upside Today* (July 20, 1998) said that "Yahoo . . . built a natural Internet brand through its simple desire to satisfy customers."

Yahoo! grew in the late 1990s through a series of acquisitions of other companies. Among some of the more notable purchases were Four11 in 1997 (whose product, RocketMail, would ultimately become Yahoo!Mail) and ClassicGames.com (which would ultimately be the foundation for Yahoo!Games). Also during this time the company developed Yahoo!Pager, an instant messaging service that would be renamed Yahoo!Messenger a year later. The company also created the MyYahoo! site, which allowed personalization of a user's front page. All of these innovations and acquisitions led to the Yahoo! stock closing at an all-time high of $118.75 per share on January 3, 2000.

Yahoo attracts hundreds of millions of users every month through its innovative technology and engaging content and services, making it one of the most trafficked Internet destinations and a world class online media company. Yahoo!'s vision is to be the center of people's online lives by delivering personally relevant, meaningful Internet experiences. With headquarters in Sunnyvale, California, the company has grown to almost 14,000 employees with offices in more than 25 countries, regions, and territories.

We believe deeply in the use of multidisciplinary teams to help steer IP strategy and policy issues broadly affecting Yahoo! We utilize an intellectual property board of directors that meets several times a year. The team is comprised of senior company leaders from areas such as engineering, research and development, legal, branding, business development, corporate strategy and finance. Our goal is to proactively look at our pipeline and overall strategies to ensure that we are fully capitalizing on our intellectual assets. Yahoo! is a technology and media company and not just a search engine. Our intellectual assets are some of our most important assets. We are constantly evaluating what has value, what it will cost, how it is branded, and how long it can last.

Further, we utilize an intellectual property asset management group, which is responsible for managing the intellectual assets of the company and continually evaluating our IP strategies.

Part of innovation is making mistakes, and the culture must embrace this philosophy to work.

We continue to focus on building a more cooperative process with business partners, working together toward our common goal and building a strong Yahoo! brand.

J. SCOTT EVANS,
Senior Legal Director,
Global Brands and Trademarks, Yahoo!

Intel

Headquartered in Santa Clara, California, Intel operates 200 facilities worldwide, including a presence in Argentina, China, Costa Rica, Mexico, Israel, Ireland, Russia, and other countries. Among the largest customers served are Hewlett-Packard and Dell. Some of the company's leading products include microprocessors, Bluetooth chipsets, motherboard chipsets, flash memory, and network interface cards.

The company got its start in 1968, when Gordon E. Moore and Robert Noyce joined forces. At its inception, the founders wanted to name the company Moore Noyce, but soon realized that this sounded like "more noise," something they did not want associated with their products. Settling on NM Electronics for about a year, the company purchased the rights for a different name, calling themselves "Intel" Corporation, a coined term derived from "integrated electronics." At its inception, the company employed 12 employees. In 1971, the company went public.

Also in 1971, Intel released its first-ever microprocessor, the item that made modern handheld calculators, personal computers, cash registers, and traffic lights possible. By 1980, the company had grown to employ nearly 15,000 people. In 1983, the company reached the $1 billion mark in sales for the first time, and by the end of the decade, the company was heading for a period of growth as the main supplier of the PC industry. In 1991, the company launched its long-running Intel Inside advertising campaign in over 130 countries around the world in order to gain public brand loyalty and awareness of the company. Also during this time, the company diversified by introducing products in the network, communications, and personal conferencing product lines. In 1999, Intel was added to the Dow Jones Industrial Average. In 2005, Intel created a "structure and efficiency team" to lead a corporate restructuring effort, resulting in a more nimble, agile company, able to quickly respond to customer demands and changing market conditions. Today, Intel is an American-based Fortune 500 company that employs over 83,000 people and is growing strong.

> Intel has worked very hard to create programs that foster innovative thinking and build leadership potential in our management. In fact, I just completed a leadership program that is designed to take 25 leaders in the company off-site for a three-week program. We work in multi-disciplinary teams to solve a real business problem the company is facing. Through this program, we learn to think in new ways and foster creativity to solve the problem. We eliminate fear of failure to think about all possible solutions. The result has been powerful new ideas coming from this program, as well as developing a culture of company leaders who embrace this philosophy.
>
> It doesn't come naturally to everyone to work as a team. Inherently many people would rather sit at their computer and e-mail everyone rather than pick up the phone or go to a meeting. As company leaders, we must foster and facilitate direct communication. You never know who is going to have

the idea that changes everything. If we aren't facilitating open communication and working as a team, then we might miss it.

RUBY ZEFO,
Director, Trademarks and Brands, Intel

Scripps Networks Interactive

Scripps Networks Interactive is a newly formed company spun out of the E.W. Scripps Company and is widely considered one of the most forward-thinking media companies in the world. It houses brands such as Food Network, Home and Garden Television (HGTV), Do-It-Yourself (DIY) Network, Fine Living, and Great American Country (GAC) and has partnered with such celebrities as Martha Stewart, Rachael Ray, Emeril, Candice Olson, and more.

Beginning as a traditional media company, in 1878 Edward Willis Scripps started the Cleveland Penny Press with $10,000 borrowed from family members. In 1883, he acquired control of the *Cincinnati Penny Post* and changed the name of this paper to *The Cincinnati Post* in 1890. That same year he started *The Kentucky Post*. This trend of acquisitions and start-up papers continued until 1908, when Edward Scripps retired (although he still managed the company until 1920).

Upon his retirement in 1920, Edward Scripps made Robert P. Scripps the editor and Roy W. Howard the business manager. In 1922, the company created the motto, "Give light and the people will find their own way." Over the next 60 years, the company continued its growth, aggressively acquiring and merging with other media companies of all kinds, including newspaper and radio companies. Particularly in the 1980s, the company began buying and creating cable television systems as a way to generate revenue that was not dependent upon advertising. In 1988, the E.W. Scripps Company made its initial stock offering.

By 1990, the company's common stock began trading on the New York Stock Exchange. This marked the beginning of a decade of change for the company, as it begins to focus attention on more electronic media outlets as opposed to newspapers. In 1994, the company created HGTV. In 1997, the company purchased the Food Network. In 1998, the DIY channel was created, and in 2000, plans for the Fine Living channel were announced (the station started in 2002). In 2004, the company purchased Summit

America TV, Inc. and GAC. Next, the company purchased Shopzilla in 2005.

As a result of the change in focus, the board of directors for the E.W. Scripps Company authorized a split in October, 2007. The goal was to create two publicly traded companies. The first would be focused on the growing national television lifestyle brands and global Internet services and would be named Scripps Networks Interactive. The other would focus on innovation and the local media market, Scripps Network. The split officially took place on June 30, 2008. Today, Scripps Networks Interactive, Inc. is head-quartered in Cincinnati, Ohio. The company currently employs nearly 2,000.

> We are a company of brands and that is a relatively new way of thinking for us. Many people may not know who Scripps Networks Interactive is, and that's okay. What's important is that they know our brands and that we do everything we can to ensure that we continue to deliver on our promise to our consumers and our advertisers in building and maintaining our brand. As a company we strive to ensure that everyone is constantly working toward those common goals with a shared vision that our brands are our business. We believe that good ideas can come from anywhere and try to foster a culture where those ideas can be heard and percolate to the top.
>
> A.B. Cruz III,
> Executive Vice President, Chief Legal Officer, and
> Corporate Secretary, Scripps Networks Interactive, Inc.

Libby Persyk Kathman (LPK)

LPK is an international design agency with a proven track record in Building Leadership Brands. By integrating strategy, design, and innovation, LPK leverages relevant consumer, shopper, and market insights to create value, sustain leadership, and transform businesses.

The agency's portfolio of category-leading brands and long-term client relationships attracts some of the best and brightest creative minds in the world. LPK's combination of strategic skills, creative disciplines, and cross-cultural perspectives results in brand-building innovation across media, geography, and time.

With a presence in North America, Europe, and Asia, LPK is the world's largest employee-owned design agency. LPK has developed and managed brand design franchises for some of the world's most successful businesses, including Gillette, Pampers, Olay, 3M, Jim Beam, IBM, Hershey, Coleman, U.S. Bank, AT&T, Kellogg, Novartis, Samsung, PepsiCo, and Kraft Foods.

LPK has been recognized by *The Wall Street Journal* as a "Winning Workplace" and by *Inc.* magazine as "one of America's Fastest Growing Private Companies."

> Every expression leaves an impression. Make every impression count.
>
> Benton Sauer,
> Vice President of Innovation, LPK

> At the heart of our process is collaboration. We want the right stimulus, which means we need the right people from various disciplines for the formation of good ideas.
>
> Bill Thiemann,
> Executive Vice President, and
> Benton Sauer,
> Vice President of Innovation, LPK

Northlich (Brand Engagement Agency)

Founded in 1949, the company has perfected the approach to brand engagement from a behavioral point of view. This approach allows the company to understand the underlying motivations and behaviors of consumer in making brand choices. This understanding led it to the trademarked approach of Rehavior, a proprietary approach to understanding and changing the existing behaviors of the consumer and establishing new behaviors that have a direct impact on brand growth. This process has been incorporated into the advertising strategy. The company's current slogan is "The Rehavior Movement Starts Here."

Northlich serves several prominent brands, including *American Greetings, Birds Eye Foods, Long John Silver's, White Castle, Macy's totes/ Isotoner,* and the *Ohio Lottery Commission.* Other prominent clients include *Procter & Gamble, Duke Energy,* and the *Ohio State University Medical Center.*

Headquartered in Cincinnati, Ohio, Northlich specializes in changing the perceptions and behavior of the consumer. The company currently has over 150 employees in three offices around the United States.

> Our agency believes that in order to generate sustainable brand growth we must affect not only consumer perception, but consumer behavior. Many agencies will stop at perception, but we go one step further, changing existing consumer behaviors and even establishing new behaviors that lead to new and stronger relationship with brands. We call this process Rehavior.
>
> We don't believe behavior change is affected by simple changes in communications strategies and marketing alone, and as such our ideas don't automatically begin or end there. We look at all aspects of brand engagement from product innovation to brand experience. Each of these can play a critical role in affecting shifts in perceptions, paradigms, preference and ultimately behavior.
>
> Our Northlich "rehaviorists" engage people by creating brand experiences that are relevant and meaningful to them, ultimately inspiring and motivating both action and ongoing interaction.
>
> KATHY SELKER,
> President, Northlich

Interbrand (Branding Consultancy)

Interbrand Corporation is headquartered at 103 Fifth Avenue in New York City. It currently has 40 offices around the globe and is the world's largest brand consultancy.

Founded by John Murphy in 1974, the company, originally called Novamark, was a product-naming consultancy. One of the company's first clients was the Post Office in London, England. Then, in 1979, the company helped the automaker British Leyland to name a new vehicle, the Metro. The car went on to become the bestselling small car in the United Kingdom. Around this same time, the company was encouraged by another client, Mars Candy Company, to open a New York office. Agreeing to do so, the firm made the move and changed its name to Interbrand. The company also changed its business focus to branding.

Expansion continued during the 1980s as other international offices were opened in Tokyo, Japan; Frankfurt, Germany; Milan, Italy; Los Angeles, California; and Melbourne, Australia. Each branch location offered the branding services of graphic design, naming, and legal searches. Also during this decade, the company named the brands Prozac; HobNobs, a popular English biscuit; and the new Pepsi lemon-lime drink, Slice.

Perhaps the company's biggest success was its innovative creation of the concept of brand evaluation. To achieve this, the firm announced its innovative proprietary Economic Value Added methodology for brand evaluation in 1987. This approach includes analyzing the brand's market, conducting a study of the brand's earnings, and applying a multiple to brand earnings based on the quality of the brand. In 1988, the company conducted its first evaluation of 50 different brands for one of the United Kingdom's largest flour millers, and the following year it evaluated Pillsbury in preparation for sale to another company.

The 1990s saw both change and continued success for the company. While serving such clients as Breyers ice cream, Compaq computers, and IBM, the founder decided to sell the company to Omnicom in 1993. The following year, the company expanded, opening a branch in South Korea, and also acquired Schecter Group in New York. In 1996, the company opened an office in Japan, added another in Switzerland, and purchased another New York firm. The era of expansion has continued, and the company has continued to do work for such powerhouse clients as Nationwide, PricewaterhouseCoopers, Procter & Gamble, and The Kroger Co. (via the acquisition of Cincinnati-based Hulefeld Associates).

The company has also serviced Heinz ketchup, Subway, Cooper Mini automobiles, Samsung, and Nikon. It has also done work for the Girl Scouts of America and created the name, logo, and identity system for Thomson Reuters. The company also releases its rankings of the best global brands on a yearly basis via *BusinessWeek* magazine.

BrandWizard is one of its most innovative programs. Under this program, businesses are aided in managing their identities across various markets. Among those services offered is a web-based system allowing clients to house and distribute their brand guidelines, currently used by Mercedes, ExxonMobil, AT&T, Hyatt, Barclays, *National Geographic*, General Motors, American Cancer Society, Office Depot, and more.

A great brand will be a pillar of the company and serve as a distinctive essence of what the company or product means to the consumer. Understanding this principle is a shift that has occurred in the last 5–10 years.

JEROME MCDONNELL,
Senior Trademark Consultant, Interbrand

The Entrepreneurial Journey

Each of the companies we researched began as an entrepreneurial journey of building a brand. Some of these companies began more than a hundred years ago; some less than 10 years ago. Whether you are an entrepreneur building your brand or a brand manager inside a large organization, the lessons these leaders have shared about how to work as a team can help you implement multidisciplinary thinking in your organization and your work. The insights we discovered about the value of designing intellectual property strategy into the creative brand development process can have a profound impact on the bottom line and the long-term return on investment.

Every company begins an entrepreneurial journey. The excitement of building a brand and maintaining a brand can be rediscovered with each new project when working as a team.

Brand Capitol and Brand Maestro

*B*rand Rewired offers a unique approach to an otherwise age-old topic: offering marketing and branding executives what will help them differentiate their campaign and create long-term economic value by intersecting what they do with a powerful intellectual property strategy.

The timing for this book could not be more perfect. In the aftermath of an economic crisis and continued budget constraints, this approach taps into cost savings coupled with leveraging the explosive value of intellectual assets.

Brand Rewired offers a new way of thinking, flipping over the innovation pipeline and creating real value by intersecting creative, business, and intellectual property.

The next book in this series will feature the unique branding and innovation coming out of one of the quiet branding capitals in the world—Ohio. Yes, that's right. This Midwest region is responsible for more innovative and creative thought than you may realize. We'll study the innovative successes that were spawned there and talk to the leaders who helped make it happen.

Did You Know?

- Some of the biggest advertisers in the world are based in Ohio.
  - Procter & Gamble
  - Macy's
  - The Kroger Co.

- The Limited
- Victoria's Secret
- Abercrombie & Fitch
- Ohio is the fifth largest state for headquarters of Fortune 500 companies with 27 companies, just behind Illinois, California, New York, and Texas.
- Cincinnati ranks sixth in the country for number of companies in the Fortune 500 per million residents and fourth for the Fortune 1000.
- According to the "100 Leading National Advertisers" database compiled by *Advertising Age,* Procter & Gamble Co. is the number one advertiser in the world, spending an estimated $5,230,100,000 on advertising in 2007, more than Walt Disney Co., Coca-Cola Co., Nike, IBM, Apple, and Gap Inc. combined (see http://www.brandminute.com/my_weblog/2008/08/proctor-gambl-1.html).
- LPK, based in Cincinnati, Ohio, is the largest employee-owned brand design agency in the world, employing 350 worldwide.
- The University of Cincinnati's College of Design, Architecture, Art and Planning (DAAP) is consistently ranked as one of the most prestigious design schools in the United States and the world.
- The University of Cincinnati embeds a top College of Design Architecture, Art and Planning in a comprehensive research University with Colleges of Business, Engineering, Law, Nursing, Arts and Sciences and a College Conservatory of Music.
- The University of Cincinnati created the first Co-Operative Education program in the country over 100 years ago.
- The University of Cincinnati has created the Live Well Collaborative (LWC) as a model for corporations and universities, specializing in R&D projects for the 50+ market (http://www.livewellcollaborative.org/newsite/index.php/mission).
- Bob Evans started in Ohio and is currently a $1.7 billion company with over 709 full-service restaurants and a complete line of retail food products under several brands, including Bob Evans Restaurant, Owens, and Mimi's Café (see http://bobevans.stg.sbc-adv.com/ourcompany/Default.aspx).

- Wendy's, a company that began in Columbus, Ohio, is often considered to have had one of the top advertising campaigns ever, with its "Where's the beef?" campaign in 1984 (see http://adage.com/century/campaigns.html; http://www.allbusiness.com/marketing-advertising/marketing-advertising-overview/12352488-1.html).
- The value of Iams, headquartered in Dayton, Ohio, grew from $100,000 in 1970 to $900 million in 1999.
- The Limited, Inc., based in Columbus, Ohio, is one of the largest corporate collections of specialty apparel retailers in the United States, owning such titans as Victoria's Secret and Abercrombie & Fitch.
- The Food Network (Scripps Networks Interactive, headquartered in Cincinnati, Ohio) is seen in more than ninety million households.

In *Brand Capitol*, we will highlight why and how Ohio is often referred to as the cradle of branding and the secrets to these companies' success. In the final book in this series, *Brand Maestro*, we will detail the process of facilitating collaborative multidisciplinary teams in the innovation and branding space and provide more details about how to design in intellectual property strategy to produce more powerful results.

APPENDIX
A

Discussion Questions

As you move into evaluating how to implement the ideas discussed, answer a few questions about your organization.

Innovation

- How does your company foster innovation?
- Who is involved in the innovation process and/or creation of new ideas?
- Do you or others in your organization find incentive financially or by awards for innovation?
- How do you measure the success of an innovation?
- What is the greatest challenge you face with innovation?
- How does your company tap into consumer insights in the innovation process?

Multidisciplinary Teams

- Does your company utilize multidisciplinary teams?
- What are the biggest obstacles in forming interdisciplinary teams?
- How can you foster collaboration and interdisciplinary teams?
- Are there incentives for working as a team?
- Are there roadblock or barriers?

Branding

- How do you define a great brand? What are the characteristics?
- How do you measure the ROI of a branding campaign?
- What is the most important trend in branding that you see?
- When does the crossover from R&D to branding occur in your company?
- Do you evaluate how you can protect your product designs, packaging, or campaigns through intellectual property?
- When you develop new branding and marketing campaigns, do you consider how to protect each aspect as intellectual property? When is that considered?
- Are you more concerned about avoiding lawsuits or ensuring that you can prevent others from infringing on your branding campaign? Is one more important than the other?
- When do you involve lawyers in the discussion? Why at that time?

Annual Planning and Intellectual Property

- When you prepare your annual projections and business plan, do you consider how you are using your brand, the value of your brand, or your branding campaign?
- When you prepare your projections and annual business plan, do you consider how you are using or protecting your intellectual property or the use of your intellectual property portfolio?
- Is the value of intellectual property primarily considered when evaluating a possible merger, acquisition, or sale or is it considered at other times?
- Do you prepare an intellectual property strategy? Who is involved? Is it in writing?
- Do you factor into your planning and budgeting potential exposure to lawsuits?
- How do you manage risk associated with intellectual property?
- If you could change one thing about the process, what would it be?

B

About the People Interviewed in This Book

Joanne Bischmann, Vice President, Licensing and Special Events, Harley-Davidson

 Joanne Bischmann guides the worldwide licensing strategy as well as overseeing the planning for Harley-Davidson's special events including the popular anniversary events. She and her licensing team are responsible for all licensed products, which enhance the Harley-Davidson experience for current customers and bring the brand to new customers. The products are distributed through the Harley-Davidson worldwide dealer network and select stores that reach new customers.

Bischmann has been with Harley-Davidson for 19 years and has held various positions within the marketing organization. She also serves on the Harley-Davidson Museum Advisory Board.

Upon joining the company in 1990, she served as manager, advertising and promotions, director of marketing, and VP of marketing before accepting her current position in 2007.

Prior to joining Harley-Davidson, Bischmann was employed in advertising at Hoffman, York and Compton of Milwaukee, Wisconsin.

Bischmann graduated from the University of Colorado, Boulder, with a bachelor of arts degree in communication.

A.B. Cruz III, Executive Vice President, Chief Legal Officer, and Corporate Secretary, Scripps Networks Interactive, Inc.

 A.B. Cruz, 51, is the executive vice president, chief legal officer, and corporate secretary for Scripps Networks Interactive, Inc. Prior to assuming this position, Cruz was executive vice president and general counsel for the E.W. Scripps Company (Scripps). Cruz joined Scripps in March 2004.

As the company's chief legal officer, Cruz is responsible for managing the company's legal function across all of its entertainment and interactive enterprises. He also oversees the company's internal audit and corporate secretary functions.

Cruz came to Scripps from BET Holdings Inc., where he was vice president, deputy general counsel, and assistant secretary. He played a leading role in BET's $3 billion merger with Viacom in 2001. Before joining BET, Cruz practiced law at several law firms in Washington, D.C., including the law firm of Wiley, Rein & Fielding where his practice focused primarily on telecommunications matters, including mergers and acquisitions involving media and communications companies, and the regulation of wireless cable, commercial and private land mobile radio, paging, and satellite services.

Before entering the legal profession, Cruz was a senior staff engineer with ARINC Research in Annapolis, Maryland, where he supported the development of various weapon systems for the U.S. Navy. He was also responsible for his department's marketing efforts. Prior to joining ARINC Research, Cruz served on military active duty for seven years as a naval officer.

Cruz is a rear admiral in the U.S. Navy Reserve and is currently serving as deputy commander, U.S. Naval Forces Southern Command and deputy commander, U.S. 4th Fleet.

Cruz is on the board of directors of the Minority Corporate Counsel Association and the American Red Cross-Cincinnati Area Chapter. He is also a director and audit committee member for the Cincinnati Symphony Orchestra. He also serves on the United States Tennis Association's audit committee.

Cruz received his juris doctorate from Catholic University's Columbus School of Law. Cruz also holds a master of business administration degree from the University of Maryland and a bachelor of science degree from the United States Naval Academy. He is a member of the District of Columbia, New York, Pennsylvania, Ohio (corporate status), and U.S. Supreme Court bars.

Inger Eckert, Chief Counsel, Intellectual Property, International Paper Company

Inger H. Eckert is the chief counsel of International Paper Company with global accountability for the strategic acquisition, management, licensing, and enforcement of the company's intellectual property as well as legal advisor to the company's technology organization. Prior to joining International Paper, Ms. Eckert was with Owens Corning, where she served in a similar role as director of intellectual property for over ten years. Her legal career began in the Office of General Counsel at Ford Motor Company after having worked as a product test and design engineer in Ford's Electronics Division. Ms. Eckert is the current president of the Association of Corporate Patent Counsel and serves on the board of directors for the National Inventors Hall of Fame Foundation.

Heidi Emanuel, Senior Innovation Officer, General Mills

Heidi Emanuel leads collection of small "catalyst" teams that support General Mills divisions in leveraging innovation best practices. Examples of a few of the catalyst teams include i-Squad: cross-functional team that facilitates new product teams in identifying new growth opportunities. They are trained in "best in class" approaches for doing this, such as creative problem solving, facilitation, improvisational acting, and so on. x-Squad: cross-functional team that helps General Mills capitalize on external innovation. They develop the tools and methods necessary to enable teams to identify and access innovation outside of General Mills. In-Market Experimentation: a team that focuses on helping GMI experiment in a market very early to gain valuable real-world learning. The team works at the intersection of sales and new product development teams so they can facilitate this early learning as well as identify strategies that will help GMI grow with its customers.

Emanuel has been with General Mills for more than 20 years and held positions in a variety of functions prior to leading S&I, including traditional research and development, marketing/new business development, and corporate strategy.

Emanuel holds a graduate degree in food science and nutrition from the University of Minnesota.

J. Scott Evans, Senior Legal Director, Global Brands and Trademarks, Yahoo!

 J. Scott Evans received his undergraduate degree from Baylor University and his juris doctor cum laude in 1992 from the Louis D. Brandeis School of Law at The University of Louisville. He served as corporate counsel for Fruit of the Loom, where he was responsible for managing the international intellectual property portfolios for Fruit of the Loom and its associate companies, The B.V.D. Licensing Corporation, Gitano, Pro Player, and Salem Sportswear, Inc. In November 1996, he joined Adams Evans P.A. where he continued to concentrate his practice in the areas of trademark, copyright, unfair competition and Internet law. In November 2007, Evans joined the legal team at Yahoo! Inc., where he serves as a senior legal director, global brands and trademarks.

Evans served on the five-member drafting committee that assisted the staff at the Internet Corporation for Assigned Names and Numbers (ICANN) with the drafting of the Uniform Dispute Resolution Policy (UDRP) and the Rules of Procedure for the UDRP. He also served as member of the Implementation Recommendation Team charged with proposing possible solutions for brand protection in new gTLDs. He is an active member of the International Trademark Association (INTA), where he is a member of the board of directors. Evans currently serves as a special advisor to the Internet Committee at INTA and is currently president of the Intellectual Property Constituency (IPC) the body that participates on behalf of trademark and copyright owners in the ICANN policy process. He was recently voted as one of the 50 Most Influential People in IP by *Managing Intellectual Property* magazine. He frequently lectures on trademark and Internet policy issues as well as domain name dispute resolution.

Steve Goers, Vice President of Open Innovation and Investment Strategy, Kraft Foods

Steven Goers is vice president of open innovation and investment strategy for Kraft Foods. In this role, he leads open innovation initiatives for Kraft focused on levering external innovation as an enabler to accelerate growth. He is also responsible for RD&Q knowledge management, intellectual property, and external investment strategies. Goers assumed this assignment in 2007.

Goers has 27 years of R&D experience at Kraft Foods. Over his career, he has held several leadership positions across the R&D organization including strategy, product development, new technology discovery, and breakout new product development supporting the beverages, coffee, desserts, and cereal businesses in both the United States as well as Banbury, England.

Goers holds a PhD in biochemistry and microbiology from Rutgers University, New Jersey; an MS in biology from SUNY Binghamton, New York; and a BA in biology from Gordon College, Wenham, Massachusetts.

Jacqueline Leimer, Distinguished IP Practitioner in Residence, Chicago-Kent College of Law, Former VP and Associate General Counsel, Kraft Foods, Former President, International Trademark Association

Jacqueline Leimer is a practitioner-in-residence with Chicago-Kent's program in intellectual property law and also directs IIT's new interdisciplinary master's program in intellectual property management and markets.

Leimer most recently was vice president and associate general counsel, global intellectual property, at the world headquarters of Kraft Foods, in Northfield, Illinois, with responsibility for the overall management of intellectual property law issues worldwide from 2005 to 2009. She started her affiliation with Kraft Foods in 1996 as chief trademark counsel.

Prior to joining Kraft Foods, Leimer was a partner at Kirkland & Ellis in Chicago, concentrating on trademark, copyright, and advertising law matters. She also has 10 years of in-house intellectual property experience with the Quaker Oats Company. She was president of the International Trademark Association in 2004 and served for many years as a director of that organization. She was appointed by U.S. Secretary of Commerce Carlos Guitterez to serve on the Trademark Public Advisory Committee to provide oversight to the U.S. Patent and Trademark Office from 2006 to 2009. She is a frequent speaker on intellectual property issues.

Leimer is admitted to practice before the Supreme Court of the United States, the United States Federal Court for the Northern District of Illinois, and the Illinois state courts.

Leimer graduated from Valparaiso University School of Law, where she was editor-in-chief of the *Valparaiso University Law Review*. She also earned a BA in psychology from Valparaiso University.

Gregg Marrazzo, Vice President and Chief Counsel, Intellectual Property and Global Marketing, Kimberly-Clark

Gregg Marrazzo is vice president-chief counsel, Intellectual Property and Global Marketing of Kimberly-Clark Worldwide, Inc., with responsibility for corporate patent, trademark, and copyright matters. In addition, Marrazzo and his team handle all general legal work for the chief marketing officers' organization. Marrazzo joined Kimberly-Clark in 1998 and has held positions of increasing responsibility since that time. Currently, he is a vice president and member of the board of directors for the International Trademark Association, the largest organization of brand owners in the world.

Before joining Kimberly-Clark, Marrazzo worked for Bausch & Lomb, Inc., where he served as senior counsel trademark and general divisional counsel for the Ray-Ban sunglasses business.

During the course of his career, Marrazzo has worked extensively in the consumer product arena, having dealt with such diverse products and services as cosmetics, eyewear, entertainment, sports franchises, publishing, and apparel.

Marrazzo is a frequent speaker on advertising, marketing, branding, and related issues.

Marrazzo is a graduate of St. John's University and received his law degree from Pace University School of Law.

Jerome McDonnell, Senior Trademark Consultant, Interbrand

Jerome McDonnell is senior trademark consultant with Interbrand's New York verbal identity team. He leads the office's trademark prescreening practice, and he is responsible for the research and risk analysis of names, taglines, and logos.

McDonnell believes that the objective of screening is to do more than "knock out" candidates; rather, it serves to inform the creative process and provide insight and guidance when it comes to building a powerful brand.

Prior to joining Interbrand, McDonnell worked as a research analyst with the intellectual property law firm Abelman, Frayne & Schwab and as a researcher with CT Corsearch. He is a member of the International Trademark Association (INTA), has been quoted in *World Trademark Review*, and has contributed to Interbrand's book *Brand Glossary*.

McDonnell graduated from Trinity College in Dublin, Ireland with an M. Phil. in psychoanalytic theory and from Keele University with an MA in criminology.

Kyle McQuaid, Senior Vice President, J Walter Thompson

It takes a unique individual to dismiss three years of demanding pre-optometry classes to focus on a new career in advertising and marketing. That abrupt change had a lot to do with a valued internship for Kyle McQuaid at The Ohio State University in the licensing and trademarks office, led by then-Program Director Anne Chasser.

Enjoying a productive and rewarding career with WPP's J Walter Thompson Co. for more than 20 years, he has never looked back.

Manager of five JWT offices and director of marketing for seven regional advertising associations over the past two decades, McQuaid developed the unique ability to incorporate national trademarks and intellectual properties beyond traditional applications on regional and grassroots levels to enhance the brand. He is responsible for initiating several national alliances and high-profile naming rights agreements, including Ford Center in Oklahoma City.

McQuaid was hired by the Professional Golf Association of America to lead its advertising, marketing, public relations, and trademark use for the 89th PGA Championship as executive chair.

He earned his BA in journalism from Ohio State University and currently lives in Oklahoma with his wife, Tammy, and their two daughters, Regan and Bryn.

Nils Montan, Former Chief Trademark Counsel, Warner Bros., Former President, International Trademark Association and International AntiCounterfeiting Coalition

Nils Montan has practiced intellectual property law for over 30 years. He presently is of counsel to the Brazilian law firm of Dannemann Siemsen Bigler & Ipanema Moreira and the owner of the intellectual property social networking site IPAlly. com. Montan was formerly vice president, senior intellectual property counsel at Warner Bros. and is also a former president of the International Trademark Association and the International AntiCounterfeiting Coalition.

Benton Sauer, Vice President of Innovation, LPK

Benton N. Sauer, vice president, group creative director, has spent nearly two decades at LPK, supervising a wide variety of brand assignments in the food technology and lifestyle categories. Sauer is credited with providing key leadership, creative direction, and a high level of strategic consultation on initiatives for Procter & Gamble, The Hershey Company, The Kellogg Company, Hasbro, 3M, Microsoft,

IBM, Intuit, Intel, Miller, Coors, and Jim Beam Global. Sauer's proven client and creative leadership skills, as well as his contributions to new business efforts, have resulted in organic growth with a number of key LPK clients.

Sauer is the driving force behind LPK's Innoventures®, a dynamic innovation process that works to extend brand offerings and build brand business. Sauer's Innoventures process has resulted in actionable business opportunities for Procter & Gamble, The Kellogg Company, and Jim Beam Global, among others.

In addition to his professional work at LPK, Sauer has also taught as an adjunct professor at the University of Cincinnati and Northern Kentucky University, guest lecturing on brand design innovation as well as creativity training. Sauer holds a BS in graphic design from the University of Cincinnati Design, Architecture, Art and Planning program (DAAP).

Kathy Selker, President, Northlich

Kathy Selker's leadership style is a combination of straight shooter, servant leader, savvy business strategist, and mom—perfect for creating an environment that nurtures talent and creativity, is open to new ways of thinking, and puts people before things in every way that matters. Ask her, and she'll tell you that her most important job is to cultivate talented, bright, creative people and give them the room and tools they need to do their job.

Since taking over the helm, she has led a bold new vision for the agency best described by her five core values: selflessness, transparency, passion, greatness, and courage. Under Selker's leadership, these values are more than words on a page. These values have fueled bold action on her part that includes reorganizing the agency into new client-centered, cross-functional villages, establishing a dynamic new leadership team, and embarking on the agency's first-ever positioning initiative.

Selker had about eight years of increasing responsibility at Northlich after joining the agency in 2000 as chief financial officer. She was serving as chief operating officer when she took the top job in January 2008. In addition, she also has 20 years of leadership and hands-on experience with major corporations such as Arthur

Anderson & Company, Federated Department Stores, and Coca-Cola Bottling Group.

Selker holds a BA in economics and an MBA from the University of Cincinnati, where she sits on the Business Advisory Council at the College of Business. She is a trustee and president of the board of the Cincinnati Ballet Company, regional director of the American Association of Advertising Agencies board of directors, member of the Cincinnati USA Regional Chamber of Commerce Agenda 360°, an executive member of the Women's Foodservice Forum, and a mentor at Oyler Elementary School.

Scott Phillips, Vice President and Trademark Practice Leader, Charles River Associates

Scott D. Phillips is vice president and head of the trademark practice group at Charles River Associates. He advises companies and counsel in transactional, tax, litigation, strategy, and financial reporting matters involving trademarks and brands, patents and technologies, copyrights and artistic properties, and business interests. His testimony experience includes federal, state, and tax court matters regarding the valuation of brands, patents, lost profits, reasonable royalties, and businesses. Phillips also assists companies and governmental agencies on IP strategy and compliance issues. These projects generally involve transfer pricing between related entities, valuation for financial reporting, or strategy assignments involving the development of IP inventories, benchmarks, and competitive assessments. He holds a BS in economics from Northern Michigan University and an MBA in finance from Michigan State University.

Gordon Smith, Professor, Franklin Pierce Law Center, and Chair, AUS, Inc.

Gordon V. Smith is chair of AUS, Inc. and distinguished professor of intellectual property management at Pierce Law, Concord, New Hampshire. He has advised clients in valuation matters for nearly 50 years. His assignments have included appraisals of nearly every type of tangible and intangible property as well as consultations relative to royalty rates, economic life, and litigation damages relating to intellectual property. Clients have included major international corporations and law firms, as well as regulatory bodies and national governments.

Smith, a graduate of Harvard University, has lectured on valuation subjects throughout the Americas, in Europe, and extensively in Asia. He has taught university-level courses at Singapore Management University and the National University of Singapore. He has conducted seminars for the IP Academy (Singapore), Chinese and Korean government agencies, the U.S. Treasury Department, and has lectured in various countries for the World Intellectual Property Organization.

He is a member of the Advisory Committee on Intellectual Property and Board of Trustees of Pierce Law, whose intellectual property curriculum is nationally recognized. Smith is a member of the International Trademark Association and the Licensing Executives Society.

His writings include many professional papers and articles that have appeared in publications worldwide. He has authored five books, published by John Wiley & Sons, Inc., including *Trademark Valuation*; *Valuation of Intellectual Property and Intangible Assets* (coauthor); and *Intellectual Property: Licensing and Joint Venture Profit Strategies* (coauthor). His most recent work is *Intellectual Property: Valuation, Exploitation, and Infringement Damages*. He also has contributed to several other Wiley intellectual property and tax reference books.

David Stimson, Chief Trademark Counsel, Kodak, and Former President, International Trademark Association

 David Stimson is chief trademark counsel for Eastman Kodak Company in Rochester, New York, with worldwide responsibility for Kodak's trademarks and copyrights. He is a graduate of Hamilton College and the University of Cincinnati College of Law. He was president of the International Trademark Association and a member of INTA's Select Committee on the Federal Trademark Dilution Act. He was a member of the Trademark Public Advisory Committee to the U.S. Patent and Trademark Office from 2000 to 2003. He has taught

courses on trademark law and Internet law at Syracuse University College of Law and the University of Cincinnati College of Law.

Bill Thiemann, Executive Vice President, LPK

Bill Thiemann, executive vice president, chief customer officer at LPK and 25-year veteran of the communications industry, is a visionary who has been instrumental in the design, management, and innovation of category-leading brand identity programs for Folgers, Millstone, Pampers, Similac, Chef Boyardee, IBM, AT&T Wireless, and Expedia. Thiemann leads the client services group, manages customer relations at every level, and plays an integral role in LPK's continued international expansion.

Thiemann is a current member of the Cincinnati Parks Board of Trustees, Employee Resource Association Board of Directors, Design Management Institute, In-Store Marketing Institute, and is a past board member of the American Institute of Graphic Arts (AIGA), Cincinnati Chapter. Thiemann holds a BS in graphic design from the University of Cincinnati Design, Architecture, Art and Planning program (DAAP).

Craig Vogel, Associate Dean, Design Architecture, Art and Planning, University of Cincinnati

Craig M. Vogel is the associate dean of Research and Innovation in the college of Design Architecture, Art and Planning (DAAP) at the University of Cincinnati (UC). He is also a professor in the School of Design with an appointment in Industrial Design. He is a fellow, past president elect and chair of the board of the Industrial Designers Society of America (IDSA). He is co-author of the book *Creating Breakthrough Products* (Prentice Hall, 2002) with Professor Jonathan Cagan. He is one of three authors of a book on innovation and organic growth, *Design of Things to Come*, released in June 2005.

During the last 25 years Professor Vogel has been a consultant to over 20 companies and advised and managed dozens of research projects and design studios collaborating with industry. He was recognized, in the 2008 Design Intelligence publication listing the best design and architecture schools, as one of the most admired design educators in the United States. He recently co-founded the Live Well Collaborative (LWC) a joint venture between UC and P&G. The LWC has four corporate members and is a non-profit organization that creates cross functional teams to design products and services for 50+ consumers. UC faculty student teams from the colleges of DAAP, Business, Medicine and Engineering work with faculty to respond to projects proposed by LWC members. To date the collaborative has worked on eight different projects including health care, yogurt, and financial advising.

His education experience includes over 20 years of teaching at all levels of undergraduate and graduate design education at the Institute of Design, IIT, The School of the Art Institute of Chicago, Carnegie Mellon University and University of Cincinnati. His areas of expertise include: Integrated New Product Development, Design Strategy, Design Studio, Design History. He has held various administrative positions prior to accepting the position of director of the CDRI in DAAP they include: co-chair of Design at The Art Institute of Chicago, associate head School of Design, co-director of the Masters of Product Development and associate dean in the College of Fine Arts at Carnegie Mellon University. Professor Vogel has conducted seminars and lectured throughout Asia and Europe. He has an MID from Pratt Institute and a BA in Psychology from Marist College.

Vince Volpi, Chair and Chief Executive Officer, PICA, a Global Anti-Counterfeiting Company

Vincent Volpi started his career in retail loss prevention, working internationally with companies such as Polo Ralph Lauren. He has also been a security consultant with ITT, a specialized claims investigator with Equifax and the Insurance Crime Prevention Institute, a secret service officer with the Franklin County Prosecuting Attorney's office, and sheriff's detective with the FCSO. He has lived and worked throughout the United States, Latin America, and Europe while consulting in loss prevention and risk management. He has authored many articles and contributed to books and research in brand protection, especially, and has lectured world-wide and at his alma mater, The Ohio State University.

Volpi specializes in the prevention of white-collar crime and the development of loss prevention programs and management systems. He has helped to reorganize troubled companies, prepared companies for public offerings, consulted on mergers and acquisitions, and designed inventory control, distribution, and information systems to increase efficiency and reduce fraud and waste.

Jeff Weedman, Vice President, Global Business Development, Procter & Gamble

P&G Vice President Jeff Weedman leads Global Business Development (GBD), which encompasses Connect+Develop (P&G's global branded approach to open innovation), mergers and acquisitions, licensing (technology and trademark), outsourcing, and so on. GBD's role is to accelerate innovation in new products and services for consumers worldwide by seeking external collaboration opportunities for world-class technology, business propositions, and brands. GBD also makes P&G's capabilities and assets available to help facilitate value creation for external companies.

Weedman's GBD group's results have been featured in numerous publications/media around the world, including *The Wall Street Journal, Associated Press, BusinessWeek, The Financial Times,* BBC Radio, and *The Economist* (Jeff accepted, for P&G, *The Economist's* 2007 first-ever Corporate Innovation award).

His P&G career includes brand management and finance roles, marketing, sales, and general manager responsibilities across well-known brands like Tide, Dawn, Folgers, and others in the United States and Canada.

Weedman's expertise has been sought for various boards and memberships, including yet2.com; Green Earth Cleaning, LLC; Glad JV (P&G's partnership with Clorox); European Industrial Research Management; Swiss Precision Diagnostics JV (P&G's partnership with Inverness Medical); Agile Pursuits (P&G's franchising subsidiary); and he is an advisor for CincyTech and the University of Michigan's Samuel Zell & Robert H. Lurie Institute for Entrepreneurial Studies. He has also been a featured keynote speaker at many open innovation conferences around the globe. He is a member of the Licensing Executives Society (LES) and is a Certified Licensing Professional.

A native of Anderson, Indiana, he received his BA at Albion College (Michigan) and completed his MBA at the University of Michigan. He resides in Cincinnati, Ohio, with his wife, son, and daughter.

Bob Wehling, Former Global Marketing Officer, Procter & Gamble

Bob Wehling likes to be known first and foremost as a grandfather of 24, a father of six wonderful ladies, and a husband to Carolyn.

Born in Chicago, he graduated from Denison University in 1960 and immediately joined Procter & Gamble in Cincinnati, Ohio. Except for three years in the U.S. Air Force, he spent his entire career at P&G, retiring after 41 years in 2001. He spent his career in a variety of marketing, public relations, government relations, and foundation positions. He was elected a senior vice president in 1994 and his last position was global marketing and government relations officer.

Wehling has been actively involved in education and children's issues at the local, state, and national levels for over 39 years. These activities range from serving as president of a local board of education to the founding of the Cincinnati chapter of the Children's Defense Fund. He co-founded a statewide business/education coalition in Ohio. Many of his efforts relate to quality teaching. He serves on the National Commission for Teaching and America's Future and was vice chair of the National Board for Professional Teaching Standards until retiring in 2003.

He is currently serving as senior advisor and board of directors member for the James B. Hunt Jr. Institute for Educational Leadership and Policy Development. The institute is committed to ensuring that all politicians of all parties in all states have the latest and best data and research available to them as they frame policies for education and early childhood programs.

Wehling is currently serving as chair of Common Sense Media. This group provides parents across the United States with the best, most objective reviews of movies, television shows, and video games so they can make appropriate decisions for themselves and their families.

While Wehling was at Procter & Gamble, he worked with Andrea Alstrup of Johnson and Johnson to found the Family Friendly Television Forum. This group, which now includes over 40 major advertisers, has been working to help ensure that families have more good options for programs to watch together, especially in the early prime-time hours.

Until recently, he served as co-chair of the Ad Council's Advisory Committee on new campaigns. He continues to serve as a member of this committee.

Bob and Carolyn reside at Riverview Farm in Augusta, Kentucky, where Carolyn raises Tennessee Walking Horses.

Ruby Zefo, Director, Trademarks and Brands, Intel

 Ruby Zefo is director of trademarks and brands legal at Intel Corporation. Zefo manages the team responsible for all legal aspects of Intel's trademark practice worldwide, including clearance, licensing, prosecution and enforcement. She began her legal career at the law firm of Fenwick & West, specializing in intellectual property and general commercial litigation. In 1996 she joined Sun Microsystems, Inc., specializing in marketing, licensing, and trademark law. She joined Intel in 2003.

Zefo is a member of the International Trademark Association (INTA) board of directors for the 2008–2010 term, and chairs the board's Audit Committee. In addition, she chairs the INTA Enforcement Committee and serves on the Policy Development and Advocacy (PDA) Executive Council. She is also a frequent speaker on international trademark clearance, prosecution, licensing, and enforcement practices.

Zefo has a BS in business administration from the University of California at Berkeley and a JD from Stanford Law School.

APPENDIX C

Mutual Nondisclosure Agreement

Mutual Confidentiality and Nondisclosure Agreement

THIS AGREEMENT is made this _____ day of _____, 2010, by and between _____ and _____ (the *"Company"*), and _____ (the *"Consultant"*).

Recitals

WHEREAS, Company is developing certain business concepts, themes, or ideas (the *"Project"*);

WHEREAS, Consultant desires to consult with Company in furtherance of the development and deployment of the Project; and

WHEREAS, in furtherance of the development of the Project, Company and Consultant may mutually provide to one another Confidential and Proprietary Information and both parties desire to protect such Confidential and Proprietary Information;

NOW THEREFORE, in consideration of the promises, mutual promises, and covenants hereinafter contained, the receipt and adequacy of which is hereby acknowledged, the parties hereto, intending to be legally bound hereby, agree as follows:

Agreement

1. Purpose. This Agreement is made for Company and Consultant to freely share Confidential and Proprietary Information for the purpose of exploring opportunities to enter into a partnership, joint venture, alliance, independent contractor, or other relationship to develop and deploy in the marketplace the Project.

2. Confidential & Proprietary Information Definitions. Confidential and Proprietary Information shall be held in strictest confidence by the Receiving Party. Neither the nature nor the content of any Confidential Information shall, directly or indirectly, be disclosed to others or used by the Receiving Party without the prior written permission of the Disclosing Party. "Disclosing Party" shall mean the party disclosing Confidential Information; "Receiving Party" shall mean the party to which Confidential Information is disclosed. "Confidential Information" means products, formulas, formulations, ingredients, research, designs, samples, ideas and inventions, discoveries, equipment, manufacturing methods and processes, computer programs, techniques, strategies, methods of distribution, capabilities, systems, technology, specifications, customers, marketing and sales information, business plans, financial data, consumer data, employees, or any other private matters or trade secrets of a party and its subsidiaries and affiliates regardless of whether such information is disclosed directly or indirectly in written, oral, or visual form. Except as provided in Section 5, all information disclosed by a party during the term of this Agreement shall be deemed the Confidential and Proprietary Information of the Disclosing Party, irrespective of the source or true ownership of such information.

3. Further Agreements for Use of Confidential Information. The parties agree to disclose Confidential Information only to officers, employees, and agents (*"Affiliates"*) with a need-to-know and to secure the compliance of such officers, employees, and agents with this Agreement. The Receiving Party will ensure that any of its Affiliates receiving Confidential Information be bound in writing by an obligation of confidentiality no less protective of such Confidential Information than the terms herein. Each party to this Agreement shall cause and enforce, at its sole cost and expense, that each Affiliate of such party that becomes a Receiving Party hereunder will comply with the provisions of this Agreement. The Receiving Party assumes responsibility and liability for all disclosures to third parties made by its Affiliates in breach of this Agreement. The Receiving Party agrees that immediately upon discovery of any unauthorized use or disclosure of Confidential Information or any other breach of this Agreement by it, or its Affiliates, the

Receiving Party will notify the Disclosing Party and cooperate in every reasonable way to help the Disclosing Party regain possession of the Confidential Information and prevent any further unauthorized use and disclosure.

Receiving Party may disclose Confidential Information of Disclosing Party only for purposes of the joint activity of the parties.

4. No Transfer of Intellectual Property Rights. Nothing in this Agreement shall be construed to grant to Receiving Party any title, ownership, intellectual property right, or license in the Confidential Information of Disclosing Party, and Receiving Party acknowledges that it does not acquire any such title, ownership, intellectual property right, or license under this Agreement. Nothing in this Agreement shall be construed as an obligation of either party to enter into a contract, subcontract, or other business relationship with the other party. Consultant acknowledges that while ideas themselves may not be protected that the concept and idea of the Project are considered proprietary and trade secret information of Company. In furtherance thereof, Consultant may not utilize any Confidential Information to engage in any activities directly or indirectly competitive with the purpose and scope of the Project for a period of one year (1) after the termination of this Agreement.

5. Exclusions. The term "Confidential Information" shall not include, and this Agreement shall not apply to: (i) any information known prior to such disclosure free of any obligation to keep it confidential, and (ii) any information that is within the public domain at the time of disclosure or that subsequently enters the public domain through no action on the part of the Receiving Party or any person having an obligation of confidence to the receiving party respecting such information.

6. Return of Confidential Information. If the Disclosing Party shall request the return or elimination of Confidential Information (which shall be described with reasonable particularity in such request), within fifteen (15) calendar days after the receipt of such request, the Receiving Party shall return the same (including all copies thereof to the Disclosing Party), if in tangible form, and/ or delete or erase such specified Confidential Information from its computer systems. Upon the expiration or termination of this Agreement, the Receiving Party shall promptly, but in any event within thirty (30) calendar days following the date of expiration or termination, return any and all Confidential Information and copies thereof in tangible form that it received from the Disclosing Party and is held in its possession, custody, or control, and each party shall delete or erase all such Confidential Information from its computer systems.

7. Discovery. If the Receiving Party hereto becomes subject to a demand for discovery or disclosure of the Confidential Information of the Disclosing Party, under lawful process, the Receiving Party shall give the Disclosing Party prompt notice for the demand prior to furnishing the Confidential Information demanded.

8. Injunctive Relief & Remedies. In the event that Receiving Party breaches this Agreement, damages may not provide an adequate remedy for Disclosing Party. Therefore, the parties acknowledge that, in the event of a breach or threat of breach, Disclosing Party may be entitled to seek injunctive relief, in addition to any other relief or damages available at law or in equity. In such event, if the Disclosing Party is Company, it shall have the right to bring any such action in Hamilton County, Ohio, and Consultant hereby consents to such jurisdiction.

In addition to the above remedy, in the event Consultant breaches Section 4 of this Agreement, Company shall be entitled to compensatory damages including lost profits or opportunities and punitive damages from Consultant.

9. Severability. In the event any provision of this Agreement shall be held invalid or unenforceable by any court of competent jurisdiction or by operation of law, then this Agreement shall be construed as if not containing the particular provision or provisions hereof held to be invalid or unenforceable, and the rights and obligations of the parties shall be construed and enforced accordingly.

10. Governing Law. This Agreement and all actions arising under it shall be governed by Ohio law. Any suit regarding this Agreement must be brought in a court of competent jurisdiction in Hamilton County, Ohio.

11. No Waiver. The rights and remedies under this Agreement exist in addition to, and not in lieu of, any rights and remedies which either party may be entitled to under applicable law. The enforcement of any right or remedy under this Agreement will not be deemed to be a waiver of any other right or remedy which either party may possess in law or equity. No waiver of any right by either party under this Agreement will be deemed a continuing waiver, and either party may demand strict compliance with this Agreement at any time.

12. Assignment. This Agreement may not be assigned in whole or in part without the other party's prior written consent.

13. Term. This Agreement shall remain in effect until the Consultant is no longer actively engaged by the Company; provided, however, that the confidentiality obligations and provisions contained in paragraph 4 herein shall continue for so long as the Disclosing Party treats the Confidential Information as confidential. Except as otherwise expressly agreed by the parties in writing, upon termination of this Agreement, Receiving Party shall (a) immediately cease using Confidential Information of Disclosing Party, (b) promptly return to Disclosing Party or destroy all media received from Disclosing Party that contain Confidential Information of Disclosing Party, (c) destroy all other copies of Disclosing Party's Confidential Information in Receiving Party's possession or control, and (d) upon written request, promptly certify in writing Receiving Party's compliance with the terms of this Article.

14. Continuing Effect. This Agreement shall be binding on, and inure to the benefit of, the Parties and their respective heirs, executors, administrators, legal representatives, successors, and permitted assigns.

15. Entire Agreement. This Agreement constitutes the entire Agreement between the parties. This Agreement shall not be modified or amended except by a written instrument duly executed by both parties hereto.

The parties hereto have duly caused this Mutual Confidentiality and Nondisclosure Agreement to be executed as of the date first above written.

CONSULTANT:

_____

Name: _____

Date: _____

Address: _____

COMPANY:

_____

Name: _____

Date: _____

Address: _____

A P P E N D I X

Sample Questionnaire for Planning Sessions

- What is the problem and opportunity being presented to the company or that you are facing?
- What internal resources are available or not available?
  - Strengths
  - Weaknesses
- External Factors Influencing the Company
  - What government/regulations are impacting the business and this problem or opportunity?
  - How is the economy/access to capital impacting the business and this problem and opportunity?
  - What cultural/societal issues will impact the business and this problem and opportunity?
  - What technological changes or issues will impact the business and this problem and opportunity?
- Competitive Analysis
  - Who are the traditional competitors?
  - Who are nontraditional or indirect competitors?
  - What concerns you most about competitors?
  - What concerns you least about competitors?

- Market Analysis
  - Who are the stakeholders (customers, consumers, employees, shareholders, other owners, vendors)?
  - What do they want and need and why?
  - What is their daily experience like?
  - How do we know?
- What will mean success in quantitative and qualitative means to you?
- What are your goals for this problem/opportunity?
- What are your concerns about this problem/opportunity?

E

Team Meeting Agenda

- Goal of the Project
  - Company goal
  - Group goals
  - Rewards and incentives to the team
- Intellectual property exploitation and protection
- Time constraints, deadlines
- New issues impacting the plan
- Report by all group members on their progress, new issues, or concerns
  - Identification of any issues based upon each report for group discussion
    - Group discussion to bring resolution or determine further homework needed to make better decision on any issues identified
- Celebration of successes achieved
- Identification of new opportunities
- Next steps

Sample Intellectual Asset Strategy Document

Objectives—What is the objective of the project? This must be stated in clear but quantifiable terms. Only one verb should be used per objective. The project may be a licensing opportunity, new campaign, new brand, new product, new technology, joint venture, etc.

Measurement Tools—How will success be defined? When will it be measured?

Strategies—What will be done, why, and by when?
  Development—How will the brand and IP be created and tested?
  Exploitation—How will the IP be fully leveraged in the marketplace?
  Risk Management—How will lawsuits and risk be avoided?
  Enforcement—How will the IP be protected?

Tactics—What are the details of how it will get done?

Incentives—What incentives will lead team members to work collaboratively?

Return on Investment—How will this impact cash and revenue and produce a return on investment for the company?

List of Trademarks

Mark	Serial No.	Registration No.	Registration Date	Owner of Mark
Amazon One Click	75413262	2264368	1999— July 27	Amazon Technologies, Inc.
Apple	73120444	1078312	1977— Nov 29	Apple Inc.
Barnes & Noble	73165683	1138704	1980— Aug 12	Barnes & Noble College Bookstores, Inc.
Big Mac	72456124	1126102	1979— Oct 16	McDonald's Corporation
Brand Rewired	77738100			Jennifer C. Wolfe
Brand Maestro	77738092			Jennifer C. Wolfe
British Airways	73548596	1408939	1986— Sep 9	British Airways, PLC
Chanel (Symbol)	71205469	0195359	1925— Feb 24	Chanel Inc.

(Continued)

Mark	Serial No.	Registration No.	Registration Date	Owner of Mark
Coach (Symbol)	73052296	1070999	1977—Aug 09	Coach, Inc.
Coach (Symbol)	78007596	2626565	2002—Sep 24	Coach, Inc.
Coca-Cola	71254696	0238145	1928—Jan 31	The Coca-Cola Company
Disney	73239204	1162727	1981—July 28	Disney Enterprises, Inc.
Doritos	72198545	792667	1965—July 13	Frito-Lay North America, Inc.
Drum Roll For Twentieth Century Fox Film Corporation	74629287	2000732	1996—Sep 17	Twentieth Century Fox Film Corporation
Dyna	74648443	1953344	1996—Jan 30	H-D Michigan, LLC
Christian Louboutin Shoes Unique Red Sole	77141789	3361597	2008—Jan 1	Christian Louboutin, Individual
Egg McMuffin	72423174	0973602	1973—Nov 20	McDonald's Corporation
The Enthusiast	71440508	0388621	1941—Jul 1	H-D Michigan, LLC
Ferrari	72286257	0862633	2009—Dec 31	Ferrari S.P.A. Corporation

(*Continued*)

Mark	Serial No.	Registration No.	Registration Date	Owner of Mark
Fotomat Building Shape	73523639	1362512	1985— Sep 24	Enliven Marketing Technologies Corporation
Four Seasons	73198201	1195412	1982— May 11	Four Seasons Hotels Limited
Fuddruckers Restaurant	73382882	1298164	1984— Sep 25	Fuddruckers, Inc.
Goldfish	73705855	1640659	1991— Apr 09	PF Brands, Inc.
Google	7554461	2884502	2004— Sep 14	Google Inc.
Harley-Davidson	71531113	0508160	1949— Apr 5	H-D Michigan, LLC
Harley	73373047	1352679	1985— Aug 6	H-D Michigan, LLC
Harley Owners Group	73558408	1455825	1987— Sep 1	H-D Michigan, LLC
Herbal Essences	74304800	1794598	1993— Sep 28	Clairol Incorporated
Herman Miller Furniture	72120212	0733770	1962— Jul 03	Herman Miller, Inc.
Herman Miller Product Design	76002312	2754826	2003— Aug 26	Herman Miller, Inc.
Herman Miller Product Design	76594225	3105591	2006— Jun 20	Herman Miller, Inc.

(Continued)

Mark	Serial No.	Registration No.	Registration Date	Owner of Mark
Herman Miller Product Design	75010956	2716843	2003—May 20	Herman Miller, Inc.
Hermes Bags	76700119			Hermes International
Hermes Bags	75662712	2447392	2001—May 01	Hermes International
Hermes Bags	75662709	2447391	2001—May 01	Hermes International
Hermes Bags	74336038	1806107	1993—Nov 23	Hermes International, Inc.
Hermes Bags	76700120			Hermes International
HGTV	75379503	2205702	1998—Nov 24	Scripps Networks, LLC
H.O.G.	76670549	3296168	2007—Sep 25	H-D Michigan, LLC
Hooters Restaurant	73775646	1557380	1989—Sep 19	Hooter's, Inc.
iMac	76366151	2876046	2004—Aug 24	Apple Inc.
iMac	77402800			Apple Inc.
Intel (Tones)	75332744	2315261	2000—Feb 08	Intel Corporation
iPhone	77303256	3457218	2008—Jul 01	Apple Inc.
iPhone	77218458			Apple Inc.
iPhone	77303049	3475327	2008—Jul 29	Apple Inc.
iPod	78925932	3365816	2008—Jan 08	Apple Inc.

(*Continued*)

Mark	Serial No.	Registration No.	Registration Date	Owner of Mark
iPod	78661217	3341214	2007—Nov 20	Apple Inc.
iPod	77389539			Apple Inc.
KFC Secret Recipe	73426450	1303969	1984—Nov 06	KFC Corporation
Kleenex (Box Design)	72103407	0744081	1963—Jan 22	Kimberly-Clark Corporation
Kleenex (Box Design)	78578374	3341048	2007—Nov 20	Kimberly-Clark Corporation
Kodak (Logo Color Scheme)	72391056	0936068	1972—Jun 20	Eastman Kodak Company
Louis Vuitton (Symbol)	71313984	0286345	1931—Aug 25	Vuitton & Vuitton
The Guide	Common Law			Limited Brands
Make Today Delicious—Kraft	77604121			Kraft Foods Global Brands, LLC
McNuggets	73269313	1276402	1984—May 01	McDonald's Corporation
MGM Lion Roar	73553567	1395550	1986—June 3	Metro-Goldwyn-Mayer Lion Corp.
Mr. Clean	78938614	3346268	2007—Nov 27	The Procter & Gamble Company

(Continued)

Mark	Serial No.	Registration No.	Registration Date	Owner of Mark
NBC (Chimes)	72349496	0916522	1971—Jul 13	The National Broadcasting Company, Inc.
Nike (Swoosh)	73302503	1325938	1985—Mar 19	Nike, Inc.
Nokia Default Ringtone	75743899	2413729	2000—Dec 19	Nokia Corporation
Nordstrom	73409518	1281000	1984—June 5	NIHC, Inc.
Owens Corning (Pink Insulation)	73247707	1439132	1987—May 12	Owens Corning Intellectual Capital, Llc
Overstock	75805940	25503246	2001—Oct 30	Overstock.com, Inc.
Pillsbury Doughboy "Giggle"	76163189	2692077	2003—Mar 1	The Pillsbury Company, LLC
Post-it Notes (Yellow)	75610586	2402722	2000—Nov 07	Minnesota Mining and Manufacturing Company AKA 3M
Qualitex (Green)	74013732	1633711	1991—Feb 05	Qualitex Company

(Continued)

Mark	Serial No.	Registration No.	Registration Date	Owner of Mark
Reese's	73072495	1074163	1977—Sep 27	Hershey Chocolate and Confectionery Sugar Corporation
Revolution	75577016	2834717	2004—Apr 20	Revolution
Ritz-Carlton	73142343	1094823	1978—June 27	Ritz-Carlton Hotel Company
Rolls-Royce	71359008	325195	1935—June 11	Rolls-Royce Motor Cars
Softail	73454630	1344224	1985—Jun 25	H-D Michigan, LLC
Sportster	72350554	0912532	1971—Jun 8	H-D Michigan, LLC
Tide	71489826	424339	1946—Oct 1	The Procter & Gamble Company
Tiffany's	73350181	1251356	1983—Sep 19	Tiffany (NJ) LLC
Time Magazine (Cover)	73144703	1106087	1978—Nov 14	Time, Incorporated
Tony the Tiger	75160545	2136777	1998—Feb 17	Kellogg Company Corporation
White Castle Building	74280325	1808813	1993—Dec 07	White Castle System, Inc.

(Continued)

Mark	Serial No.	Registration No.	Registration Date	Owner of Mark
Yahoo! (Yodel)	75807526	2442140	2001—Apr 10	Yahoo! Inc.
Yamaha Motor Corporation (Arc of Water Flowing)	74321288	1946170	1996—Jan 09	Yamaha Motor Co., Ltd.

References

Ad Agencies vs. Consultancies: Weighing the Difference. *Brandchannel,* April 21, 2009, http://www.brandchannel.com/forum.asp?bd_id=4.

Advertising and Marketing on the Internet. Federal Trade Commission, *Bureau of Consumer Protection,* September 2000, p. 1, 3–4, 6.

Albee, Ardath. Customer Content vs. Marketing Content. *Marketing Interactions Blog,* August 23, 2009, http://marketinginteractions.typepad.com/marketing_interactions/2009/08/23/.

Allen, Robert C. Soap Opera. *The Museum of Broadcast Communications.* September 25, 2009, http://www.museum.tv/eotvsection.php?entrycode=soapopera.

Amazon.com, Inc. http://www.fundinguniverse.com/company-histories/Amazoncom-Inc-Company-History.html (Accessed November 17, 2009).

American Legion Auxiliary National Public Relations. American Legion Auxiliary Public Relations Handbook. 2005, http://www.legion-aux.org/Files/PRHandbook.pdf#search=%22patent%2055398%20legion%22.

Anderson, J. Scott. Painstaking Semantics: Selecting Website Trade Dress Elements to Survive a Copyright Preemption Challenge. 7 *J. Marshall Rev. Intell. Prop. L.* 97 (2007).

Anderson, Nate. Ten Years of Futility: COPA Finally, Truly Dead. ARSTechnica, January 21, 2009, http://arstechnica.com/tech-policy/news/2009/01/ten-years-of-futility-copa-finally-truly-dead.ars.

Ante, Spencer E. At Amazon, Marketing Is for Dummies. *Business Week Special Report 100 Best Global Brands,* September 28, 2009, p. 53–54.

AOL Time Warner Inc. http://www.fundinguniverse.com/company-histories/AOL-Time-Warner-Inc-Company-History.html (Accessed October 15, 2009).

Apple Computer, Inc. http://www.fundinguniverse.com/company-histories/Apple-Computer-Inc-Company-History.html (Accessed October 15, 2009).

Apple, Inc. (AAPL): Profile. http://finance.yahoo.com/q/pr?s=AAPL (Accessed October 15, 2009).

Aranoff, Stephen and Robert FitzPatrick. Not Invented Here: A Concept Whose Time Is Passed: Opening the Creative Process to New Ideas Can Open New Doors. *Digital Output,* October 2003, http://www.digitaloutput.net/content/contentct.asp?p=414.

BabyCenter, LLC. 22 Surprising Facts about Birth in the United States. August 2009, http://www.babycenter.com/0_22-surprising-facts-about-birth-in-the-united-states_1372273.bc.

Banks, Howard. General Electric: Going with the Winners. *Forbes,* March 26, 1984, p. 97.

Barrett, William, Christopher Price and Thomas Hunt. *iProperty: Profiting from iDeas in an Age of Global iNnovation.* Hoboken, NJ: John Wiley & Sons, 2008.

Bellafante, Gina. A 'Satire' of a Classic Fails to Amuse Hermès. *New York Times,* B8, August 12, 2003, http://www.nytimes.com/2003/08/12/nyregion/a-satire-of-a-classic-fails-to-amuse-the-august-house-of-hermes.html?pagewanted=1.

Benson, Joseph, Rob Levinson and Drew Allison. The Solution to Brand Dilution. *BrandPapers,* http://www.brandchannel.com/papers_review.asp?sp_id=1256.

Bhupendra, Khanal. Brand Dilution Is as Important as Brand Enhancement. *Business Analytics,* July 7, 2007, http://www.bhups.net/2007/07/brand-dilution-is-as-important-as-brand.html.

Blumenstein, Rebecca, Geoffrey Fowler, Jared Sandberg, Rebecca Buckman, and Kris Maher. Beyond Global. *The Wall Street Journal,* March 21, 2002, p. B6.

Bone, Daniel. Contagious Case Study—Doritos. *Contagious Magazine.*

Booth, Steve. Doritos Superbowl Commercial Needs Extras. Message to Southern Ohio Filmmakers Association. October 13, 2009. E-mail.

Bracey, Hyler, Jack Rosenblum, Aubrey Sanford and Roy Trueblood. *Managing from the Heart.* New York: Delacorte, 1990.

Brady, Diane and Kerry Capell. GE Breaks the Mold to Spur Innovation. *Business Week,* April 26, 2004, p. 88.

Brand Equity. 28 September 2009, http://en.mimi.hu/marketingweb/brand_equity.html.

Brand Equity. 28 September 2009, http://www.answers.com/topic/brand-equity.

Brandjacking and Cybersquatting Continues to Grow. *Traverselegal Attorneys & Advisors,* July 3, 2009, http://tcattorney.typepad.com/domainnamedispute/2009/07/markmonitor-has-reported-that-the-online-abuse-of-leading-brands-rose-in-2008-the-report-stated-that-80-of-the-abusive-si.html.

Brandt, Richard, Otis Port and Robert D. Hof. Intel: The Next Revolution. *Business Week,* September 26, 1988, p. 74.

Brayer, Elizabeth. *George Eastman: A Biography.* Baltimore: Johns Hopkins University, 1996.

British Airways PLC. http://www.fundinguniverse.com/company-histories/British-Airways-PLC-Company-History.html, Accessed January 25, 2010.

British Airways: History and Heritage. http://www.britishairways.com/travel/history-and-heritage/public/en_gb, Accessed January 25, 2010.

Brief Guide to Intellectual Property in the United Arab Emirates.

Brogan, Chris. How Content Marketing Will Shake the Tree. August 6, 2008, http://www.chrisbrogan.com/how-content-marketing-will-shake-the-tree/.

Brown, Mike. What Are You Passionate About? *Blogging Innovation,* August 3, 2009, http://www.business-strategy-innovation.com/2009/08/what-are-you-passionate-about.html.

Brymer, Chuck and Interbrand. What Makes Brands Great? *Brandchannel,* http://www.brandchannel.com/papers_review.asp?sp_id=359.

Bughin, Jacques R. How Companies Can Make the Most of User-Generated Content. *The McKinsey Quarterly,* August 2007.

Burnette, Ed. Cisco Lost Rights to iPhone Trademark Last Year, Experts Say. January 12, 2007, http://blogs.zdnet.com/Burnette/?p=236.

Burns, Greg. Has General Mills Had Its Wheaties? *Business Week,* May 8, 1995, pp. 68–69.

Byrne, John and Joseph Weber. The Shredder: Did CEO Dunlap Save Scott Paper—Or Just Pretty It Up? *Business Week,* January 15, 1996, pp. 56–61.

Byrne, John. Jack: A Close-Up Look at How America's #1 Manager Runs GE. *Business Week,* June 8, 1998, pp. 90–95, 98–99, 102, 104–06, 110–11.

Campbell-Smith, Duncan. *The British Airways Story: Struggle for Take-Off.* London: Coronet Books: Hodder and Stoughton, 1986.

Carlson, W. Bernard. *Innovation as a Social Process: Elihu Thomson and the Rise of General Electric, 1870–1900.* New York: Cambridge University Press, 1991.

Casagrande, Tom. 7th Circuit's Recent Trade Dress/Reverse Passing Off Decision (follow-up). *Likely to be Confused: The Softer Side of IP Law,* August 17, 2005, http://secondarymeaning.blogspot.com/2005/08/7th-circuits-recent-trade-dressreverse.html.

Cenar, Kara. Proactive and Effective Ownership of Intellectual Property—It Does Make a Difference. January 1, 2002.

Chadwick, James M. Two Recent Decisions Reframe the DMCA Discussion. *Intellectual Property Law,* October 7, 2008, http://www.intellectualpropertylaw blog.com/archives/copyrights-two-recent-decisions-reframe-the-dmca-discus sion.html.

Chaplinsky, Susan and Graham Payne. Methods of Intellectual Property Valuation. Charlottesville, VA: University of Virginia Darden School Foundation, 2002.

Cherenson, Michael. Member Bulletin: New FTC Guidelines Explained. Message to Jennifer Wolfe. October 7, 2009. E-mail.

Chesbrough, Henry. *Open Business Models: How to Thrive in the New Innovation Landscape.* Boston: Harvard Business School, 2006.

Chesbrough, Henry. *Open Innovation: The New Imperative for Creating and Profiting from Technology.* Boston: Harvard Business School, 2003.

Cip, Benjamin. Are You Violating the FTC Rules? June 25, 2009, http://benjamin cip.com/beware-of-the-ftc/.

Clark, Tim. Inside Intel's Marketing Machine. *Business Marketing,* October 1992, pp. 14–19.

Collins, Douglas. *The Story of Kodak.* New York: Abrams, 1990.

Collins, Jim and Jerry Porras. *Built to Last: Successful Habits of Visionary Companies.* New York: HarperCollins, 1997.

Collins, Jim. *Good to Great: Why Some Companies Make the Leap . . . and Others Don't.* New York: Harper Business, 2001.

Company Profile for General Mills, Inc. (GIS). http://zenobank.com/index.php?s ymbol=GIS&page=quotesearch (Accessed October 15, 2009).

Conducting an IP Audit—Checklist: Identifying Your IP. http://www.iptoolbox .gov.au/default.asp?action=article&ID=167.

Considerations Relevant to Best Mode. MPEP 2165.01.

Cordery, Brian and Danielle Onona. The Potential Pitfalls of Registering Product Shapes as TMs. *Magazine of Intellectual Property & Technology,* August 10, 2005, http://www.ipfrontline.com/depts/article.asp?id=5125&deptid=4.

Corke, Alison. *British Airways: The Path to Profitability.* New York: St. Martin's, 1986.

Corporate Information: Google: Google Milestones. http://www.google.com/corporate/history.html (Accessed October 15, 2009).

Crouch, Dennis. The Rising Importance of Method Claims. *PatentlyO*, September 7, 2009, http://www.patentlyo.com/patent/2009/09/the-rising-importance-of-method-claims.html.

Cummings, Betsy. Beating the Odds. *Sales & Marketing Management*, March 2002, pp. 24–29.

Cybersquatting and the UDRP: The US and .com Lead the Way. *Traverselegal Attorney & Advisors*, March 18, 2009, http://tcattorney.typepad.com/domain namedispute/2009/03/cybersquatting-and-the-udrp-the-us-and-com-lead-the-way.html.

Cybersquatting the Social Networks: A New Trademark Risk. *Traverselegal Attorneys & Advisors*, April 23, 2009, http://tcattorney.typepad.com/domainnamedispute/typosquatting_domain_names/.

D'Alessandro, David. *Brand Warfare: 10 Rules for Building the Killer Brand.* New York: McGraw-Hill, 2001.

A Danish Toymaker Puts It Together in the U.S. *Business Week*, September 6, 1976, pp. 80, 83.

David Rapp. Inventing Yahoo! *American Heritage*, http://www.americanheritage.com/events/articles/web/20060412-yahoo-internet-search-engine-jerry-yang-david-filo-america-online-google-ipo-email.shtml, 2006.

Davis, Julie L. and Suzanne S. Harrison. *Edison in the Boardroom: How Leading Companies Realize Value from Their Intellectual Assets.* New York: John Wiley & Sons, 2001.

Daye, Derrick and Brad VanAuken. Top 100 Brands Wield Power over S&P 500. April 30, 2009, http://www.brandingstrategyinsider.com/2009/04/.

Deal, Terrence and Allan Kennedy. *Corporate Cultures: The Rites and Rituals of Corporate Life.* N.P.: Addison-Wesley, 1982.

Delain, Nancy Baum. The Intellectual Property Audit. *LesNouvelles*, Vol. 38, No. 4, December 2003, p. 193.

DictionaryOne. Domain Name Registration FAQ. http://www.directoryone.com/domain_name_registration_faq.htm.

Digital Journal Staff. Copyright and the Mouse: How Disney's Mickey Mouse Changed the World. *Digital Journal*, October 6, 2004, http://www.digitaljournal.com/article/35485.

Dobrusin, Eric and Ronald Krasnow. *Intellectual Property Culture.* New York: Oxford, 2008.

Dodge, Don. User-Generated Content Sites Are Building Huge Communities. March 27, 2006, http://dondodge.typepad.com/the_next_big_thing/2006/03/user_generated_.html.

Domain Name Disputes Have Doubled Since 2003. *Royal Pingdom*, December 30, 2008, http://royal.pingdom.com/2008/12/30/domain-name-disputes-have-doubled-since-2003/.

Doritos Fan Trumps Advertising Professionals and Wins $1 Million Super Bowl Advertising Challenge. February 2, 2009, http://www.fritolay.com/about-us/press-release-20090202.htm.

Drucker, Peter. *Management: Tasks, Responsibilities, Practices.* New York: Harper & Row, 1974.

The Drucker Centennial. *Harvard Business Review,* November 2009.

Dunn, Michael K. The Google Book Digitization Settlement: The Fair Use Question Remains. *Intellectual Property Law,* December 8, 2008, http://www.intellectu alpropertylawblog.com/archives/copyrights-the-google-book-digitization-settlement-the-fair-use-question-remains.html.

Durkin, Tracy-Gene and Julie D. Shirk. Design Patents and Trade Dress Protection: Are the Two Mutually Exclusive? *Journal of the Patent and Trademark Office Society,* October, 2005.

Dyer, Davis, Frederick Dalzell and Rowena Olegario. *Rising Tide: Lessons from 165 Years of Brand Building at Procter & Gamble.* Boston: Harvard Business School, 2004.

Eastman Kodak Co. (EK): Profile. http://finance.yahoo.com/q/pr?s=ek (Accessed October 15, 2009).

Eastman Kodak Company. http://www.fundinguniverse.com/company-histo ries/Eastman-Kodak-Company-Company-History.html (Accessed October 15, 2009).

Edelman, Sandra. Proving Your *Bona Fides*—Establishing Bona Fide Intent to Use Under the U.S. Trademark (Lanham) Act. *The Trademark Reporter: The Law Journal of the International Trademark Association,* Vol 99, No. 3, 2009, p. 763.

Eisenberg, Bryan. The Value of Content Marketing. March 27, 2009, http://www .grokdotcom.com/2009/03/27/the-value-of-content-marketing/.

Elliott, Stuart. Thanks to the Web, the Scorekeeping on the Super Bowl Has Just Begun. *The New York Times,* February 6, 2007, http://www.nytimes. com/2007/02/06/business/media/06adco.html?_r=2&adxnnlx=1170866695-JT30AKfez1R%20Csnkn/hHvA&pagewanted=all.

Ellis-Christensen, Tricia. How Has the Average Age at Marriage Changed over Time? *WiseGeek,* December 17, 2009, http://www.wisegeek.com/how-has-the-average-age-at-marriage-changed-over-time.htm.

Evolution of Our Brand Logo. http://www.kodak.com/global/en/corp/history OfKodak/evolutionBrandLogo.jhtml (Accessed October 15, 2009).

Fahden, Allen. *Innovation on Demand: How to Benefit from the Coming Deluge of Change: Make Creativity Work for You and Your Company.* Minneapolis: The Illerati, 1993.

Fair, Michele. The History of Amazon.com: A History of the Worldwide Media Retailer Amazon.com. http://www.essortment.com/hobbies/historyamazonc_ ttas.htm, 2002.

Faust, Bill and Beverly Bethge. Looking Inward: How Internal Branding and Communications Affect Cultural Change. *Design Management Journal,* Vol. 14, No. 3, 2003, p. 58–59.

Feisthamel, Karen, Amy Kelly and Johanna Sistek. Trade Dress: Best Practices for the Registration of Product Configuration Trade Dress with the USPTO. 95 *The Trademark Reporter* 6, Nov.–Dec. 2005, http://home.comcast.net/~jlw28129/ TradeDress101.pdf.

Felber Jr., Robert Waller. Fender Hits Sour Note at Trademark Trial and Appeal Board. *INTA Bulletin,* Vol. 64, No. 11, June 15, 2009, p. 10.

Field, Jr., Thomas G. The Potential Pitfalls of Overlapping Design Patents and TMs. *Magazine of Intellectual Property & Technology,* August 19, 2005, http://www.ipfrontline.com/depts/article.asp?id=5328&deptid=4.

Finguerra-DuCharme, Dyan. Protecting a Web Site Design. *GC New York,* ALM Properties, 2007, http://www.wilmerhale.com/files/Publication/69b5a293-3cac-4de8-9545-71f990e8c15c/Presentation/PublicationAttachment/6c7eea91-be75-41a7-b702-7bfb048ffde5/07009912070002WilmerHale.pdf.

Flignor, Paul and Orozco, David. Intangible Asset & Intellectual Property Valuation: A Multidisciplinary Perspective. January 28, 2009, http://www.wipo.int/sme/en/documents/ip_valuation.htm.

Forest, Stephanie Anderson and Mark Maremont. Kimberly-Clark's European Paper Chase. *Business Week,* March 16, 1992, p. 94, 96.

Freeman, Laurie. Kimberly Holds Its Own Against Giants. *Advertising Age,* November 19, 1984.

French, Amanda L. Facebook Terms of Service Compared with MySpace, Flickr, Picasa, YouTube, LinkedIn, and Twitter. February 16, 2009, http://amandafrench.net/2009/02/16/facebook-terms-of-service-compared/.

Frieberger, Paul and Michael Swaine. *Fire in the Valley: The Making of the Personal Computer.* Berkeley, Calif.: Osborne-McGraw-Hill, 1984.

Friedman, Thomas. *The World Is Flat: A Brief History of the Twenty-First Century.* New York: Farrar, Straus and Giroux, 2005.

Fryer, William T., III. Trademark Product Appearance Features, United States and Foreign Protection Evolution: A Need for Clarification and Harmonization. 34 *John Marshall Law Review* 947–971, 2001, http://www.fryer.com/wsjmsla1.htm.

FTC Facts for Business. Federal Trade Commission, Bureau of Consumer Protection, Office of Consumer and Business Education, April 2004, p. 1.

Garfield, Bob. Top 100 Advertising Campaigns. *Advertising Age,* March 29, 1999, http://adage.com/century/campaigns.html.

Garon, Jon M. The Intellectual Property Audit: A Treasure Hunt for Hidden Corporate Assets. *Interface Tech News,* November 2001.

GE: Our History. http://www.ge.com/company/history/index.html (Accessed October 15, 2009).

General Electric Co. (GE). http://finance.yahoo.com/q/pr?s=ge (Accessed October 15, 2009).

General Electric Company. http://www.fundinguniverse.com/company-histories/General-Electric-Company-Company-History.html (Accessed October 15, 2009).

General Mills—Company Overview. http://www.generalmills.com/corporate/company/overview.aspx (Accessed October 15, 2009).

General Mills—Our History. http://www.generalmills.com/corporate/company/history.aspx (Accessed October 15, 2009).

General Mills, Inc. Company Profile. http://biz.yahoo.com/ic/10/10639.html (Accessed October 15, 2009).

General Mills, Inc.. http://www.fundinguniverse.com/company-histories/General-Mills-Inc-Company-History.html (Accessed October 15, 2009).

General Questions. *United States Patent and Trademark Office.* http://www.uspto.gov/main/faq/index.html.

Generic Domain Name Not Entitled to Trademark Registration or Protection. *Traverselegal Attorneys & Advisors,* July 28, 2009, http://tcattorney.typepad .com/domainnamedispute/2009/07/generic-domain-name-not-entitled-to-trademark-registration-or-protection.html.

Gibbons, Kevin. Why Not Selling Online Can Damage Your Brand. June 8, 2009, http://econsultancy.com/blog/3979-why-not-selling-online-can-damage-your-brand.

Gladwell, Malcolm. *The Tipping Point: How Little Things Can Make a Big Difference.* N.P.: Little, Brown and Company, 2000.

Glowacki, Jeremy. Kimberly-Clark Corp.: Accelerates Global Expansion with Scott Merger. *Pulp & Paper,* December 1995, pp. 34–35.

Goden, Robert B. Trade Dress—The Forgotten Trademark Right. July 1, 1999, http://library.findlaw.com/1999/Jul/1/128357.html.

Godin, Seth. *Purple Cow: Transform Your Business by Being Remarkable.* New York: Penguin Group, 2003.

Goldman, Eric. Downloading Music Isn't Fair Use—BMG v. Gonzalez. *Technology & Marketing Law Blog,* December 10, 2005, http://blog.ericgoldman.org/archives/2005/12/downloading_mus.htm.

Gollin, Michael. *Driving Innovation: Intellectual Property Strategies for a Dynamic World.* New York: Cambridge, 2008.

Google Inc. (GOOG): Profile. http://finance.yahoo.com/q/pr?s=GOOG (Accessed October 15, 2009).

Google, Inc., http://www.fundinguniverse.com/company-histories/Google-Inc-Company-History.html (Accessed October 15, 2009).

Gordon, John Steele. What Digital Camera Makers Can Learn from George Eastman. *American Heritage,* http://www.americanheritage.com/articles/magazine/ah/2003/5/2003_5_23.shtml, October 2003.

Gray, James. Business Without Boundary: The Story of General Mills. Minneapolis: University of Minnesota Press, 1954.

Groeneboer, Chris, Denise Stockley and Tom Calvert. A Model for Multi-Disciplinary Collaboration. *Ascilite,* December 7–10, 1997, http://www.ascilite .org.au/conferences/perth97/papers/Groeneboer/Groeneboer.html.

Groos, Caleb. Fender Guitars Denied Trademark Registration: Trademarks and Product Design. March 30, 2009, http://blogs.findlaw.com/free_enterprise/2009/03/fender-guitars-denied-trademark-registration-trademarks-and-product-design.html.

Hackney, Holt. Kimberly-Clark: No Escaping a Messy Diaper (Business). *Financial World,* April 27, 1993, p. 16.

Hammond, John Winthrop. *Men and Volts: The Story of General Electric.* Philadelphia: Lippincott, 1941.

Harley Davidson USA: From 1903 Until Now, http://www.harley-davidson .com/wcm/content/pages/h-d_history/history.jsp?locale=en_US (Accessed October 15, 2009).

Harley-Davidson, Inc. (HOG) Profile. http://finance.yahoo.com/q/pr?s=hog (Accessed October 15, 2009).

Harley-Davidson, Inc. http://www.fundinguniverse.com/company-histories/HarleyDavidson-Inc-Company-History.html (Accessed October 15, 2009).

Harris, Thomas. *Value-Added Public Relations: The Secret Weapon of Integrated Marketing.* Chicago: McGraw-Hill, 1998.

Hazleton, Lesley. Jeff Bezos: How He Built a Billion-Dollar Net Worth Before His Company Even Turned a Profit. *Success,* July 1998, pp. 58–60.

Heinrich, Thomas. Product Diversification in the U.S. Pulp and Paper Industry: The Case of International Paper, 1898–1941. *Business History Review,* Autumn 2001, pp. 467–505.

Helliker, Kevin. A New Mix: Old-Fashioned PR Gives General Mills Advertising Bargains. *Wall Street Journal,* March 20, 1997, p. A1.

Herbold, Robert J. Overcoming the 'Fiefdom Syndrome': Conquering Office Politics. October 1, 2004, http://bpmmag.net/mag/overcome_fiefdom_sydrome_1001/.

Herman Miller Announces 'Trade Dress' Protection for Noguchi and Eames Designs. May 17, 2003, http://wwwqa.hermanmiller.com/DotCom/jsp/aboutUs/newsDetail.jsp?navId=194&topicId=53&newsId=246

Hinchcliffe, Dion. How the Web OS Has Begun to Reshape IT and Business. September 6, 2009, http://blogs.zdnet.com/Hinchcliffe/?p=771.

History of Warner Bros. http://www.free-press-release.com/news/200609/1158539308.html, September 17, 2006.

The History of Yahoo! How It All Started. http://docs.yahoo.com/info/misc/history.html, 2005.

Hoffman, Ivan. Trademark Law: An Overview. 1998, www.ivanhoffman.com/trademark.html.

Hoffman, Ivan. The Protection of 'Trade Dress.' 2002, www.ivanhoffman.com/tradedress.html.

Hogan, Thom. Apple: The First Ten Years. *A&plus: The #1 Apple II Magazine,* September 1987.

Horovitz, Bruce. From Zero to Hero in 30 Seconds Flat. *USA Today,* February 1, 2002, http://www.usatoday.com/money/covers/2002-02-01-super-bowl-ads.htm#more.

Houk, Bob. Is Walmart Violating the FTC Act? August 2, 2009, http://blog.tpmaww.tpnexus.com/2009/08/is-walmart-violating-ftc-act.html.

How Amazon Cleared the Profitability Hurdle, *Business Week,* February 4, 2002.

http://www.internationalpaper.com/US/EN/index.html.

Hubbard, Douglas. *How to Measure Anything: Finding the Value of Intangibles in Business.* Hoboken, NJ: John Wiley & Sons, 2007.

Huston, Larry and Nabil Sakkab. P&G's New Innovation Model. March 20, 2006, http://hbswk.hbs.edu/archive/5258.html.

Ingham, John N., ed. Kimberly, John Alfred. *Biographical Dictionary of American Business Leaders,* Vol. II, Westport, Conn.: Greenwood, 1983.

Intel Corporation (INTC): Profile. http://finance.yahoo.com/q/pr?s=INTC (Accessed October 15, 2009).

Intel Corporation. http://www.fundinguniverse.com/company-histories/Intel-Corporation-Company-History.html (Accessed October 15, 2009).

Intel: Corporate Timeline: Our History of Innovation. http://www.intel.com/museum/corporatetimeline/ (Accessed October 15, 2009).

Interbrand Corporation. http://www.fundinguniverse.com/company-histories/Interbrand-Corporation-Company-History.html (Accessed October 15, 2009).

Interbrand: Disciplines. http://www.interbrand.com/disciplines.aspx?langid=1000 (Accessed October 15, 2009).

Interbrand: Who We Are. http://www.interbrand.com/about_us.aspx?langid=1000 (Accessed October 15, 2009).

InternationalPaperCo.(IP):Profile.http://finance.yahoo.com/q/pr?s=ip(Accessed October 15, 2009).

International Paper Company. http://www.fundinguniverse.com/company-histo ries/International-Paper-Company-Company-History.html (Accessed October 15, 2009).

International Trademark Association. A Guide to Proper Trademark Use for Small Business Owners. New York: INTA, 2006. Print.

International Trademark Association. Managing Trademark Costs in a Down Economy—Opportunities and Obstacles for Brand Owners. *US Roundtable Program*, April 20–May 1, 2009.

International Trademark Association. A Guide to Proper Trademark Use for the Media and Public. New York: INTA, 2006. Print.

International Trademark Association. Trademark Basics: A Guide for Business. New York: INTA, 2006. Print.

Jackson, Nancy Mann. Avoiding Brand Damage—How to Determine Whether Partnerships Will Help or Hurt Your Brand. *Engagement Strategies Magazine*, Summer, 2007, http://www.motivationstrategies.com/Avoiding_Brand_ Damage.742.0.html.

Jackson, Tim. *Inside Intel: Andy Grove and the Rise of the World's Most Powerful Chip Company*. New York: Dutton, 1997.

Jeffrey, Don. Amazon.com Eyes Retailing Music Online. *Billboard*, January 31, 1998, p. 8–9.

Johnson, Wayne. Innovation 3.0: Creating the Next Level 21st-Century Innovation Ecosystem Platform. *Kauffman Thoughtbook*, 2007, http://www.kauffman.org/ advancing-innovation/innovation-3-0.aspx.

J. Walter Thompson Company (JWT) History. http://library.duke.edu/specialcol lections/hartman/guides/jwt-history.html (last modified June 29, 2006).

JWT Company Profile. http://biz.yahoo.com/ic/104/104077.html (Accessed October 15, 2009).

JWT. http://www.jwt.com/ (Accessed October 15, 2009).

Kalwarski, Tara. Investing in Brands. July 23, 2009, http://www.businessweek.com/ blogs/personal_finance/archives/2009/07/brands.html.

Karp, Scott. The User-Generated Content Myth. *Publishing 2.0*, October 26, 2007, http://publishing2.com/2007/10/26/the-user-generated-content-myth/.

Katz, Ralph and Thomas J. Allen. Investigating the Not Invented Here (NIH) Syndrome: A Look at the Performance, Tenure and Communication Patterns of 50 R&D Project Groups. *R&D Management*, vol. 12, pp. 7–19, 1982.

Kayne, R. What Is the Difference between a Design Patent and a Utility Patent? http://www.wisegeek.com/what-is-the-difference-between-a-design-patent-and-a-utility-patent?

Keller, Kevin Lane and Sanjay Sood. Brand Extensions Hold More Promise Than Peril: Parent Brands Tend to Withstand Failed Extensions. http://www.anderson .ucla.edu/x9421.xml.

Keller, Kevin. *Best Practice Case in Branding: Lessons from the World's Strongest Brands.* Upper Saddle River, NJ: Pearson Education, 2008.

Kiddon, Joan and Larry Light. *Six Rules for Brand Revitalization: Learn How Companies Like McDonald's Can Re-Energize Their Brands.* Upper Saddle River, NJ: Wharton School, 2009.

Kim, W. Chan and Renee Mauborgne. *Blue Ocean Strategy: How to Create Uncontested Market Space and Make the Competition Irrelevant.* Boston: Harvard Business School, 2005.

Kimberly-Clark: History. http://www.kimberly-clark.com/aboutus/history.aspx (Accessed October 15, 2009).

Kimberly-Clark Corporation (KMB). http://finance.yahoo.com/q/pr?s=kmb (Accessed October 15, 2009).

Kimberly-Clark Corporation. http://www.fundinguniverse.com/company-histories/KimberlyClark-Corporation-Company-History.html (Accessed October 15, 2009).

Kimberly-Clark: Company Profile. http://www.kimberly-clark.com/aboutus/company_profile.aspx (Accessed October 15, 2009).

Kimelman, John. Slash and Build: While Restructuring at Home, International Paper Is Investing Overseas. *Financial World,* April 13, 1993, p. 28.

King, Kelvin. The Value of Intellectual Property, Intangible Assets and Goodwill. October 9, 2009, http://www.wipo.int/sme/en/documents/value_ip_intangible_assets.htm.

Kirkpatrick, David. The Second Coming of Apple. *Fortune,* November 9, 1998, p. 86.

Kodak: About Kodak: History of Kodak. http://www.kodak.com/global/en/corp/historyOfKodak/historyIntro.jhtml (Accessed October 15, 2009).

Kodak: George Eastman. http://www.kodak.com/global/en/corp/historyOfKodak/eastmanTheMan.jhtml?pq-path=2217/2687/2689 (Accessed October 15, 2009).

Koller, David. Origin of the Name, Google. Stanford University, January 2004.

Kraft Foods Inc. Company Profile. http://biz.yahoo.com/ic/103/103392.html (Accessed October 15, 2009).

Kraft Foods Inc. http://www.fundinguniverse.com/company-histories/Kraft-Foods-Inc-Company-History.html (Accessed October 15, 2009).

Kraft Foods: History. http://www.kraftfoodscompany.com/about/history/index.aspx (Accessed October 15, 2009).

Kraft Replaces AIG in Dow Jones Industrial Average. http://www.usatoday.com/money/markets/2008-09-18-dow-adds-kraft_N.htm, September 18, 2008.

Krizman, Lisa. Trademark Protection for Restaurant Owners: Having Your Cake and Trademarking It, Too. *The Trademark Reporter: The Law Journal of the International Trademark Association,* Vol 99, No. 4, 2009, p. 1004.

The Kroger Co. http://www.fundinguniverse.com/company-histories/The-Kroger-Co-Company-History.html (Accessed October 15, 2009).

The Kroger Company Profile. http://biz.yahoo.com/ic/10/10864.html (Accessed October 15, 2009).

Kroger: Historic Timeline. http://www.thekrogerco.com/corpnews/corpnewsinfo_timeline_02.htm (Accessed October 15, 2009).

Kroger: History. http://www.thekrogerco.com/corpnews/corpnewsinfo_history.htm (Accessed October 15, 2009).

Krotoski, Mark. Common Issues and Challenges in Prosecuting Trade Secret and Economic Espionage Act Cases. *Economic Espionage and Trade* Secrets, Vol. 57, No. 5, November 2009, p. 2.

Ladas & Parry, LLP. Trademarks: Sounds, Colors and Scents. Revised February 16, 1996, http://www.ladas.com/Trademarks/MakingSenseTM.html.

Lafley, A.G. and Ram Charan. *The Game-Changer: How You Can Drive Revenue and Profit Growth with Innovation.* New York: Crown Business, 2008.

Laurin, Andre. Innovation 3.0: A New Way to Innovate. *Idea and Innovation Blog,* May 20, 2008, http://blog.brainbankinc.com/post/Innovation-30—A-New-Way-To-Innovate.aspx.

Laycock, George. *The Kroger Story: A Century of Innovation,* Cincinnati: The Kroger Co., 1983.

Leading Lawyers on Intellectual Property Portfolio Capitalization. *Developing an IP Strategy for Your Company.* N.P.: Aspatore, 2005.

Lego and Tyco Blocks. *New York Times,* November 15, 1988, p. D13.

Lego Taps New Markets, but Keeps an Eye on Its Image, *Brandweek,* February 8, 1993, p. 28.

Lego A/S. http://www.fundinguniverse.com/company-histories/Lego-AS-Company-History.html (Accessed November 17, 2009).

Lego: About Us—Corporate Information: Lego Timeline. http://www.lego.com/eng/info/default.asp?page=timeline (Accessed November 17, 2009).

Lee, Christina. Taking Trademark Rights seriously. Alban Tay Mahtani & de Silva, July 2004, http://www.atmdlaw.com.sg/mediacentre/pdfs/0604trademarks.pdf.

Lewis, Shari Claire. Trademark Infringement by Search Engine. Reprinted from *New York Law Journal,* October 2, 2007, http://www.rivkinradler.com/rivkinradler/Publications/newformat/200710lewis.shtml.

Lindegaard, Stefan. 10 Innovation Lessons I've Learned. *Blogging Innovation,* August 16, 2009, http://www.business-strategy-innovation.com/2009/08/10-innovation-lessons-ive-learned.html.

Lindemann, Jan and Interbrand. Brand Valuation: The Financial Value of Brands. April 21, 2009, www.brandchannel.com/papers_review.asp?sp_id=357.

Lindsay, Jeff, Cheryl Perkins and Mukund Karanjikar. *Conquering Innovation Fatigues: Overcoming the Barriers to Personal and Corporate Success.* Hoboken, NJ: John Wiley & Sons, 2009.

Linzmayer, Ronald. Apple Confidential: The Real Story of Apple Computer, Inc. http://extras.denverpost.com/books/chap0411h.htm, No Starch Press, 1999.

Lipin, Steven. Kroger Agrees to Acquire Fred Meyer. *Wall Street Journal,* October 19, 1998, p. A3.

Long, HV, Mary White and Debbie Vasen. History of Soap Operas. October 24, 2008, http://soap-operas.lovetoknow.com/History_of_Soap_Operas.

LPK: Legacy of Leadership. http://www.lpk.com/history.php (Accessed October 15, 2009).

LPK: Powerful and Enduring Brands. http://www.lpk.com/portfolio.php (Accessed October 15, 2009).

Maister, David. *Practice What You Preach: What Managers Must Do to Create a High Achievement Culture.* New York: The Free Press, 2001.

Managing One Self. *Harvard Business Review,* March—April 1999.

Manz, Charles and Henry Sims, Jr. *Super-Leadership: Leading Others to Lead Themselves.* New York: Berkley, 1990.

Marsh, Michelle Mancino, Michael Kelly and Joyce Kung. Footwear IP Protection and Litigation on the Rise. *INTA Bulletin*, Vol. 64, No. 3, February 1, 2009, p. 5.

Martin, Joanne. *Cultures in Organizations: Three Perspectives.* New York: Oxford University, 1992.

Martin, Michael. The Next Big Thing: A Bookstore. *Fortune*, December 9, 1996, pp. 168–70.

Masud, Robert. Bloggers Need to Beware of Violating FTC Deceptive Practice Standards When Making Endorsements. http://www.articlestreet.com/view/printview-35527.html.

Matheson, Julia Anne and Stephen L. Peterson. Combine and Conquer: How the Synthesis of Design Patent and Trade Dress Achieve Maximum Protection for Your Product Design. May 2009, http://www.finnegan.com/resources/articles/articlesdetail.aspx?news=74f843be-c63a-40cc-8ae0-007bc50fdd99.

Max, Theodore C. S.D.N.Y. Holds eBay Not Liable in Closely Watched Trademark Case. July 14, 2008, http://www.intellectualpropertylawblog.com/archives/trademarks-and-trade-dress-sdny-holds-ebay-not-liable-in-closely-watched-trademark-case.html.

McDaid, Damien. Evolution of the Advertising Agencies. August 2006, http://e-articles.info/e/a/title/Evolution-of-the-advertising-agencies/.

McDonald, Iain. Top 100 Most Valuable Brands in the World? Why They Got It All Wrong. May 6, 2009, http://amnesiablog.wordpress.com/2009/05/06/top-100-most-valuable-brands-in-the-world?/.

Menn, Joseph. Disney's Rights to Mickey Mouse May Be Wrong: Film Credits from the 1920s Reveal Imprecision in Copyright Claims That Some Experts Say Could Invalidate Disney's Long-Held Copyright. *Los Angeles Times*, August 22, 2008.

Merges, Robert, Peter Menell and Mark Lemley. *Intellectual Property in the New Technological Age.* New York: Aspen, 2006.

Meyer, Stuart and Rajiv Patel. The Intellectual Property Audit. *Fenwick & West*, 2005.

Michelli, Joseph A. How the Ritz-Carlton Hotel Company Is Redefining the Gold Standard. *Business Week*, Book Excerpt from *The New Gold Standard*, June 25, 2008, http://www.businessweek.com/managing/content/jun2008/ca20080625_920931.htm.

Mordden, Ethan. *The Hollywood Studios.* New York: Simon & Schuster, 1988.

The Most Valuable U.S. Retail Brands 2009. *Interbrand Design Forum*, 2009, http://www.interbrand.com/images/studies/IBDF_MostValuableRetailBrands_FINAL.pdf.

Nantus, Sheryl. Lego History. http://www.essortment.com/all/legohistory_rbco.htm, 2002.

Narisetti, Raju. For Sanders, Getting Scott Is Only the Start. *Wall Street Journal*, December 5, 1995, pp. B1, B12.

National Arbitration Forum Releases 2008 Domain Name Dispute Resolution Program Totals—Cases Span Globe and Help Trademark Holders Protect

Rights Online. *National Arbitration Forum,* March 11, 2009, http://www.adrforum.com/newsroom.aspx?&itemID=1479&news=0.

National Conference of Commissioners on Uniform State Laws. Uniform Trade Secrets Act. August 2–9, 1985, http://www.law.upenn.edu/bll/archives/ulc/fnact99/1980s/utsa85.htm.

Nelson, Kristopher. Copyright: Infringement Elements. *Notes from Law School by Kristopher Nelson,* http://lawschool.ekris.org/search/label/Intellectual%20Property.

No. 4,089 Libby, Perszyk, Kathman. http://www.inc.com/inc5000/2007/company-profile.html?id=200740890 (Accessed October 15, 2009).

Northlich: Portfolio. http://www.northlich.com/category/gallery/ (Accessed October 15, 2009).

Northlich. http://www.linkedin.com/companies/northlich (Accessed October 15, 2009).

Northlich: About Us. http://www.northlich.com/category/about-us/ (Accessed October 15, 2009).

Northlich: Rehavior. http://www.northlich.com/rehavior/ (Accessed October 15, 2009).

Northlich: Unique Capabilities. http://www.northlich.com/capabilities/ (Accessed October 15, 2009).

O'Reilly, Tim. What Is Web 2.0: Design Patterns and Business Models for the Next Generation of Software. September 30, 2005, http://oreilly.com/web2/archive/what-is-web-20.html.

O'Reilly, Tim. What Is Web 2.0: Design Patterns and Business Models for the Next Generation of Software. September 30, 2005, http://oreilly.com/lpt/a/6228.

Oates, David, The King of the Lego Castle, *International Management,* January 1974, pp. 32–36.

Ogilvy, David. *Confessions of an Advertising Man.* London: Southbank, 1987.

Ogilvy, David. *Ogilvy on Advertising.* New York: Random House, 1985.

Olins, Wally. *Corporate Identity: Making Business Strategy Visible Through Design.* Boston: Harvard Business School, 1989.

Onemargaret. Soap Opera History: Why the TV Shows Are Called 'Soap Operas'. October 29, 2008, http://www.associatedcontent.com/article/1142394/soap_opera_history_why_the_tv_shows.html?cat=39.

Orozco, David and James Conley. Shape of Things to Come: How Apple's Trademark for Its iPod Protects Its Brand—and Offers Lessons for Other Companies on How to Leverage Their Intellectual Property. *The Wall Street Journal,* May 12, 2008, p. R6.

Osborne, Richard. An Unpretentious Giant: John Georges Has Quietly Built International Paper into a Diversified $15 Billion Corporation. *Industry Week,* June 19, 1995, pp. 73–76.

Overstock.com. Naked Short Selling: Frequently Asked Questions. http://www.overstock.com/11148/static.html.

Overstock.com. History. http://investors.overstock.com/phoenix.zhtml?c=131091&p=irol-history, Accessed November 16, 2009.

Owens Corning (OC) Profile. http://finance.yahoo.com/q/pr?s=OC (Accessed October 15, 2009).

Owens Corning: A Heritage of Innovation. http://www.owenscorning.com/acquainted/about/history/ (October 15, 2009).

Palmer, Jay. No Lumbering Giant: International Paper Races to New Peaks in Earnings. *Barron's,* January 2, 1989, p. 13.

Payne, Martin. Maintaining Brand Health. *Brandloop #12,* July 2001, http://www.throughtheloop.com/knowledge/brand12.html.

Pendergrast, Mark. *For God, Country & Coca-Cola: The Definitive History of the Great American Soft Drink and the Company That Makes It.* New York: Basic Books, 2000.

Penrose, Harald. *Wings Across the World: An Illustrated History of British Airways.* London: Cassell, 1980.

Perez, Elizabeth. Store on Internet Is Open Book: Amazon.com Boasts More Than 1 Million Titles on the Web. *Seattle Times,* September 19, 1995, p. E1.

Peters, Tom. *The Pursuit of Wow! Every Person's Guide to Topsy-Turvy Times.* New York: Random House, 1994.

Phelps, Marshall and David Kline. *Burning the Ships: Intellectual Property and the Transformation of Miscrosoft.* Hoboken, NJ: John Wiley & Sons, 2009.

Pike, Christopher. *Virtual Monopoly: Building an Intellectual Property Strategy for Creative Advantage—from Patents to Trademarks, from Copyrights to Design Rights.* London: Nicholas Brealey, 2007.

Porter, Michael. *Competitive Strategy: Techniques for Analyzing Industries and Competitors.* New York: The Free Press, 1980.

Price, Mark. Brand Trek, Episode 1—Creative Development in the New Marketing World, on the Marketing Frontier. *Information Management,* February 11, 2002, http://www.information-management.com/news/4692-1.html.

Procter & Gamble Co. (P&G). Heritage. http://www.pg.com (Accessed October 15, 2009).

Procter & Gamble Co. (P&G). Profile. http://finance.yahoo.com/q/pr?s=pg (Accessed October 15, 2009).

Protecting Personal Information, a Guide for Business. Federal Trade Commission.

Pulizzi, Joe. 10 Content Marketing Tips to Start Now for 2009. http://marketing.foliomag.com/blogs/2009/10-content-marketing-tips-start-now-2009.

Qualitex Co. v Jacobson Products Co., No. 93-1577 (US March 28, 1995).

Quinn, Gene. Trademark. *IP Watchdog,* http://www.ipwatchdog.com/trademark/.

Radcliffe, Mark F. and Diane Brinson. Copyright Law. DLA Piper, 1999, http://library.findlaw.com/1999/Ja/1/241476.html.

Radcliffe, Mark F. and Diane Brinson. Patent Law. *Patent, Trademark & Trade Secret,* 1999, http://library.findlaw.com/1999/Jan/1/241479.html

Reid, Peter. *Well Made in America: Lessons from Harley-Davidson on Being the Best.* New York, McGraw-Hill, 1990.

Reilly, Robert F. Valuation of IP During a Distressed Economy—Part I. *The Licensing Journal,* September 2009, pp. 12–20.

Richardson, Gary. Brand Names Before the Industrial Revolution. 2000.

Ries, Al. Short-Term Gains and Brand Damage. *Branding* Strategy, July 30, 2009, http://www.brandingstrategyinsider.com/2009/07/recession-decisions-short-term-gains-and-brand-damage.html.

Ries, Al. Don't Damage Your Brand for Short-Term Gains in a Recession. *Marketing Watch With Kimberly,* April 9, 2009, http://marketingwatchwithkimberly.com/2009/04/09/dont-damage-your-brand-for-short-term-gains-in-a-recession.

Ritson, Mark. Counterfeits: Good for Luxury Brands? *Branding Strategy Insider*, October 3, 2007, http://www.brandingstrategyinsider.com/2007/10/fakes-can-genui.html.

Rivette, Kevin and David Kline. *Rembrandts in the Attic: Unlocking the Hidden Value of Patents*. Boston: Harvard Business School, 2000.

Roman, Kenneth. David Ogilvy: The Most Famous Advertising Man in the World. Speech at the University Club, New York, November 17, 2004, http://www.gandalf.it/m/ogilvy2.htm.

Ross, Chuck. Kraft-ing a Durable Business Model. *TVWeek*, http://www.tvweek.com/news/2008/04/krafting_a_durable_business_mo.php, April 27, 2008.

Roy, Sylvain. Introduction to IP Valuation, How Much Is Your IP Worth? 2004, http://www.ipmall.info/hosted_resources/gin/Roy_How_much_is_your_IP_worth.pdf.

Ruh, Carol. Patent/Trade Secret Complementariness. *Jorda on Trade Secrets: The Interface Between Patents and Trade Secrets*. April 23, 2008, http://www.jordasecrets.com/2008/04/patenttrade_secret_complementa.html.

Saidman DesignLaw Group. Design Patent. http://www.designlawgroup.com/tools_design_patent.cfm.

Saidman, Perry J. Note: Update on Trade Dress/Patent Conundrum: The 'Right to Copy' Doctrine.' http://www.ipo.org/AM/Template.cfm?Section=Home&Template=/CM/ContentDisplay.cfm&ContentID=22891.

Saporito, Bill. Kroger: The New King of Supermarkets. *Fortune*, February 21, 1983, p. 74.

Schickel, Richard and George Perry. *You Must Remember This—The Warner Bros. Story*. Philadelphia: Running Press, 2008.

Scola, Jr., Daniel A. and Kellyanne Merkel. Trade Dress Can Coexist Easily with Design Patent: Courts Stress That the Two Are Nonintersecting IP Subsets and Neither Can Outweigh the Other. *The National Law Journal*, Hoffman & Baron, May 31, 1999, http://www.hoffmanbaron.com/press/trade_dress.cfm.

Scripps Networks Interactive. Our Company: About. http://www.scrippsnetworksinteractive.com/our-company/about (Accessed October 15, 2009).

Scripps Networks Interactive. Our Company: History. http://www.scrippsnetworksinteractive.com/our-company/history (Accessed October 15, 2009).

Seddon, Joanna. BrandZ Top 100 Most Valuable Global Brands 2009. *Millward Brown Optimor*, 2009, http://www.millwardbrown.com/sites/optimor/Media/Pdfs/en/BrandZ/BrandZ-2009-Report.pdf.

Sheppard Mullin Richter & Hampton LLP. Consider the Venue: Significant Split among Circuits in Findings of Liability for Trademark Infringement in Metatags and Keywords. *Intellectual Property Law*, April 24, 2008, http://www.intellectualpropertylawblog.com/archives/trademarks-and-trade-dress-consider-the-venue-significant-split-among-circuits-in-findings-of-liability-for-trademark-infringement-in-metatags-and-keywords.html.

Sheppard Mullin Richter & Hampton LLP. Trade Secrets Can Be All in Your Mind. *Intellectual Property Law*, April 29, 2008, http://www.intellectualpropertylawblog.com/archives/trade-secrets-trade-secrets-can-be-all-in-your-mind.html.

A Short History of International Paper: Generations of Pride. *Generations of Pride: A Centennial History of International Paper*. International Paper Company, 1998.

Silver, Judith. *What Is Intellectual Property?: Trade Secret Law.* 2003, http://library.findlaw.com/2003/May/15/132743.html.

Silverman, Alan B. The Importance of an Intellectual Property Audit. *JOM*, 52(8) (2000), p. 56.

Simple Rules. *Brandgenuity,* April 8, 2009, http://www.brand-genuity.com/.

Sklar, Robert. *Movie-Made America.* New York: Vintage, 1994.

Smith, Gordon and Donna Suchy. IP Assets in a Flat World … That Just Got Flatter in the Global Crisis. *Landslide,* Vol. 2, No. 2, November/December 2009, p. 26.

Smith, Gordon. Fair Valuation in Singapore: Charting a Globally Competitive Framework. *Business Minds,* January 2010, p. 21.

Smith, Kimberly K. *Brave New Web: Trademark Rights in the Expanding Internet.* January 13, 2009, http://www.intellectualpropertylawblog.com/archives/internet-brave-new-web-trademark-rights-in-the-expanding-internet.html.

Smith, Steve. FTC Guidelines: Drilling the Details. *MediaPost Blogs,* February 13, 2009, http://www.mediapost.com/publications/?fa=Articles.showArticle&art_aid=100304.

Specification. *Patent* Laws, 35 U.S.C. 112, July 24, 1965.

Spector, Robert. *Amazon.com—Get Big Fast: Inside the Revolutionary Business Model That Changed the World.* N.P.: HarperCollins, 2000.

Sports Case Study: Doritos: Crash the Super Bowl. *The Marketing Arm.* September 25, 2009, http://www.themarketingarm.com/work/3/35.

Staff. Values Evolve at the Ritz-Carlton. *HOTELS Magazine,* September 1, 2006, http://www.hotelsmag.com/article/362998-Values_Evolve_at_the_Ritz_Carlton.php.

Stannard, Aaron. Five Ways to Jumpstart Your Organization's Creative Process. April 20, 2009, http://blog.smartdraw.com/archive/2009/04/20/five-ways-to-jumpstart-your-organization-s-creative-process.aspx.

Swisher, Kara. Beneath Google's Dot-Com Shell. *The Wall Street Journal,* January 21, 2002, p. B1.

Tatterson, Robert L. Why Protecting Your Brand from Counterfeiting Matters. August 13, 2008, www.industryweek.com/PrintArticle.aspx?ArticleID=17054&S.

The 15 Most Popular Web 2.0 Websites. September 8, 2009, http://www.ebizmba.com/articles/web-2.0-websites.

Top 100 Brands Outperform S&P 500 by Nearly 60 Percentage Points, WeSeed Study Shows. January 29, 2009, http://www.encyclopedia.com/doc/1G1-192797186.html.

Trademark Misuse in Facebook, Twitter, and Other Social Media Names. *Traverselegal Attorneys & Advisors,* September 21, 2009, http://tcattorney.typepad.com/domainnamedispute/2009/09/trademark-misuse-in-facebook-twitter-and-other-social-media-names.html

Treacy, Michael and Fred Wiersema. *The Discipline of Market Leaders: Choose Your Customers, Narrow Your Focus, Dominate Your Market.* N.P.: Addison Wesley, 1995.

Tregoe, Benjamin and John Zimmerman. *Top Management Strategy: What It Is and How to Make It Work.* New York: Simon & Schuster, 1980.

Two Pesos, Inc. v. Taco Caba, Inc., 112 S. Ct. 2753 (1992).

Tysver, Daniel A. Domain Name Disputes. September 25, 2009, http://www.bitlaw.com/internet/domain.html.

United Nations. United Nations Issues Wall Chart on Marriage Patterns 2000. New York: June 15, 2000, http://www.un.org/esa/population/publications/world marriage/worldmarriage2000PressRelease.htm.

United States Copyright Office. Frequently Asked Questions about Copyright . http://www.copyright.gov/help/faq/.

United States Patent and Trademark Office. Trademark FAQs. http://www.uspto .gov/faq/trademarks.jsp.

User-Generated Content Sites Breeding Ground for New Internet Security Threats Says Commtouch Trend Report. January 12, 2009, http://www.commtouch .com/press-releases/user-generated-content-sites-breeding-ground-new-inter net-security-threats-says-commt

USPTO. Types of Patents. *Description of Patent Types,* June 1, 2000, http://www.uspto .gov/go/taf/patdesc.htm.

VanAuken, Brad. The Language of Branding: 'Brand Equity'. The Harvard Business School, January 20, 2008, www.brandingstrategyinsider.com/2008/ 01/the-language–1.html.

Vazirani, Sondra, Ron D. Hays, Martin F. Shapiro and Marie Cowan. Effect of a Multidisciplinary Intervention on Communication and Collaboration among Physicians and Nurses. *American Journal of Critical Care,* Issue 14, pp. 71–77, 2005.

Verhage, Sasha. Collaboration Sessions: How to Lead Multidisciplinary Teams, Generate Buy-In, and Create Unified Design Views in Compressed Timeframes. *Boxes and Arrows: The Design Behind the Design,* September 2009, July 4, 2005, http://www.boxesandarrows.com/view/collaboration_sessions_ how_to_lead_multidisciplinary_teams_generate_buy_in_and_create_unified_ design_views_in_compressed_timeframes.

Visakowitz, Susan. Super Bowl Boosts Digital Sales for Petty and Others. *The Washington Post,* February 16, 2008, http://www.washingtonpost.com/wp-dyn/ content/article/2008/02/16/AR2008021601415_pf.html.

Von Lohmann, Fred. Required Reading for 'User-Generated Content' Sites: Io Group v. Veoh. *Electronic Frontier* Foundation, August 28, 2008, http://www.eff .org/deeplinks/2008/08/required-reading-user-generated-content-sites-io-g.

Wagner, Herbert. *At the Creation: Myth, Reality, and the Origin of the Harley-Davidson Motorcycle, 1901–1909.* Madison, Wisconsin Historical Society (2003).

Walker, Dave. Building Brand Equity through Advertising. *Ipsos-ASI The Advertising Research Company.* Research Article 5, Paper originally presented at ARF Week of Workshops, October 8, 2002.

Warner Bros. Entertainment Inc. Company Profile. http://biz.yahoo.com/ ic/103/103206.html (Accessed October 15, 2009).

Warner Bros Studios. http://www.seeing-stars.com/Studios/warnerBrosStudios .shtml (Accessed October 15, 2009).

Warner, Jack L. *My First Hundred Years in Hollywood.* New York: Random House, 1970.

Warner-Sperling, Cass and Cork Millner. *Hollywood Be Thy Name: The Warner Brothers Story.* University Press of Kentucky, 1999.

Warta, Tamara, Mary White, and Debbie Vasen. The Beginning of Soap Opera History. September 16, 2008. http://soap-operas.lovetoknow.com/Soap_ Opera_History.

Wauters, Robin. What's The Google Brand Worth These Days? $100 Billion. Probably Less. August 6, 2009. http://www.techcrunch.com/2009/08/06/whats-the-google-brand-worth-these-days-100-billion/.

Webb, Jere M. Metatags and Trademark Law: Continuing Uncertainty. *Stoel Rives, LLP,* January 1, 2004, http://www.stoel.com/showarticle.aspx?Show=3391&Print.

Weber, Cynthia Clarke. Trade Dress Basics. http://www.sughrue.com/files/Publication/a5e682a6-09e8-4fb4-8d52-f3ba796ee215/Presentation/PublicationAttachment/28d42aa1-f2c4-4516-9a6c-f84323a0b1a7/tradedress.htm.

Wesemann, H. Edward. *Creating Dominance: Winning Strategies for Law Firms.* Bloomington, IN: AuthorHouse, 2005.

What Is Content Marketing? If You're Not Content Marketing, You're Not Marketing. *Juanita 42,* http://www.junta42.com/resources/what-is-content-marketing.aspx.

White, Scott D. Brand Equity. March 16, 2005, http://ezinearticles.com/?Brand-Equity&id=20703.

Wientzen, Robert H., J. Howard Beales III and Kenneth Weaver. Screening Advertisements: A Guide for the Media. Federal Trade Commission, October 28, 2008, http://www.ftc.gov/bcp/edu/pubs/business/adv/bus36.shtm.

Will IP Provide Your Company's Next Financing. 2007, www.bpcouncil.com/viewarticle.aspx?articleID=799.

WIPR World Intellectual Property Review. N.P.: Newton Media Limited, July/August 2009.

World Intellectual Property Organization. Frequently Asked Questions. http://www.wipo.int/patentscope/en/patents_faq.html#patent_role.

World Patent Report Confirms Increasing Internationalization of Innovative Activity. Geneva, PR/2008/562, July 31, 2008, http://www.wipo.int/pressroom/en/articles/2008/article_0042.html.

Yahoo! Inc. (YHOO): Profile. http://finance.yahoo.com/q/pr?s=YHOO (Accessed October 15, 2009).

Yahoo! Inc. http://www.fundinguniverse.com/company-histories/Yahoo-Inc-Company-History.html (Accessed October 15, 2009).

Zaharoff, Howard G. Common Publishing Legal Issues and How to Avoid Them. *Inside the Minds: Winning Legal Strategies for Publishing,* 2005, http://www.mbbp.com/resources/iptech/publishing_legal.html.

About the Authors

ANNE CHASSER was named one of the 50 most influential people in the intellectual property world by *Managing Intellectual Property* magazine. As the former commissioner of Trademarks for the United States Patent & Trademark Office, Chasser achieved top-level executive experience in both government and higher education administration. Chasser developed a highly profitable licensing enterprise during her tenure as director of Trademarks and Licensing for The Ohio State University. She served as president of the International Trademark Association and continues to lead intellectual property organizations worldwide. Chasser is widely recognized as a visionary thought leader in intellectual property. Chasser currently serves as associate vice president for Intellectual Property at the University of Cincinnati. She holds a BA from the University of Dayton and MA from The Ohio State University.

JENNIFER C.WOLFE is the founder of Wolfe, LPA, one of fastest growing woman owned intellectual property and corporate counsel law firms. A few of the clients she has served includes: Kraft Foods, Scripps Networks Interactive, the Kroger Company, Luxottica Retail, Cincinnati Milacron, and emerging technology and media companies.

Wolfe is one of the only attorneys in the country also nationally accredited in public relations by the Public Relations Society of America, bringing a unique perspective to strategic creation of intellectual property portfolios. Widely known for her unique outside-the-box thinking, Wolfe is a regular contributor to a variety of national publications and speaks regularly at national conferences.

Wolfe was the first woman elected as president of the Greater Cincinnati Venture Capital Association where she served two terms and advised countless start up companies. Wolfe's firm has been named the Woman Owned Business of the Year by the Cincinnati

Regional USA Chamber of Commerce. Wolfe has been named a Leading Lawyer five times by *Cincy Magazine*, a Top Inspiring Woman by *Inspire Magazine*, one of the top 40 Under 40 professionals by the *Cincinnati Business Courier* and one of the Top 15 Women to Watch by the *Cincinnati Enquirer*.

She received her Juris Doctorate in Law and Master of Arts in Communication from the University of Cincinnati, graduated magna cume laude with a degree in journalism from Ball State University and has been trained at Harvard Law School in negotiation and mediation. Prior to founding her firm, Wolfe worked as the Marketing and Public Relations Director of a publishing company.

Index